Shakespeare Two-Thousand

Shakespeare
Two-Thousand

by
Fannie Gross

**Foreword and Additional Material
by
William-Alan Landes**

PLAYERS PRESS, Inc.
P. O. Box 1132
Studio City, CA 91614-0132

Shakespeare Two-Thousand

PLAYERS PRESS, Inc.
P.O. Box 1132
Studio City, CA 91614-0132, U.S.A.

Simultaneously Published
U.S.A., U.K., Canada and Australia

Printed in the U.S.A.

Library of Congress Cataloging-in-Publication Data

Gross, Fannie.
    Shakespeare : two-thousand / by Fannie Gross ; foreword and additional material by William-Alan Landes.
        p.   cm.
    ISBN 0-88734-626-X
    1. Shakespeare, William, 1564-1616--Examinations, questions, etc. 2. English drama--Examinations, questions, etc. 3. Questions and answers. I. Landes, William-Alan. II. Title.
PR2987.G78   1993
822.3'3--dc20

                                      92-44022
                                         CIP

FOREWORD

The two thousand questions in this book have been assembled with the idea of interesting lovers and students of Shakespeare's plays. Many answers will be known from prior reading or watching of the plays, some you will want to find by re-reading and others will possibly stump you. As a last resort, the answers are listed in the back of this book.

For simplicity, the present tense is used throughout, except for matters that occur before the action of a play begins, or a prior event in a question or in a direct quotation.

We use a capital letter, in a quotation, for a common word to indicate a new line in the original text.

In the "Play by Play Department," we follow a sequence of events. But do not anticipate this section to be an outline of each play.

The plays are taken at face value without regard to actual situations or circumstances. There is no menton of inaccuracies in historical dates, locations, or time juxtaposition.

All material selected is in accordance with "The Complete Works of William Shakespeare, The Cambridge Edition, edited by William Aldis Wright," and published by The Blakiston Company, Philadelpia.

If you need a scoring system, allow five points for each correct answer.

We hope you enjoy these Shakespearean questions and trivia.

William-Alan Landes

Contents

 (As You
Like it)

PART I

"Sundry Contemplations"

"The game's afoot!"

(*Henry V*)

1. "SUNDRY CONTEMPLATIONS"

1. What Roman warrior has survived twenty-seven wounds, only to die of the twenty-eighth, twenty-ninth, and thirtieth?

2. Name the prisoner who is too sleepy, too intoxicated, and too stubborn to be hanged.

3. Which heroine refuses to call her guardian "Mother" because she is in love with her son and does not want him for a brother?

4. Who might be "lord of the whole world" if he would agree to a pirate's suggestion that they murder his three dinner guests?

5. Whose melancholy is so contagious that a stag catches it and sheds big round tears?

6. Who knows by looking at his brother that he, himself, is a "sweet faced youth"?

7. What French lady, on approaching England for the first time, throws a diamond-studded heart-shaped "jewel" into the sea toward the shore?

8. Who bemoans, "all my glories In that one woman I have lost forever"?

9. Who is "that one woman"?

10. What Frenchman claims the English throne through his Spanish wife?

11. Who, when recommending himself for service to a King, includes among his virtues that he eats no fish?

12. In which play are there less than a dozen lines spoken by women?

13. What girl, when she is disguised as a man, adopts the name of one of her servants?
14. Who has "to Aleppo gone"?
15. Name the Emperor of Rome who flirts with one woman while he proposes marriage to another?
16. From whom do we learn that the fishes live in the sea as men do on land; the big ones eat up the little ones?
17. What girl falls in love with a man before she sees his face or knows his name?
18. Who describes an ideal commonwealth where there will be no riches, no poverty, and everyone will be idle?
19. In the quotation, "One touch of nature makes the whole world kin," what is the "one touch of nature"?
20. Without stopping to think, which is the only title that begins with the article "A"?

2. "SUNDRY CONTEMPLATIONS"

1. Whose name is suggested by his own statement, "I do lean upon justice, sir"?
2. Who pretends he is having a fit and picks the pockets of the man who helps him to his feet?
3. What superstitious man orders his wife to stand in the path of his friend so his touch can break the spell of her sterility?
4. Who incorporates the stories of King Cophetua and Julius Caesar in a love letter?
5. Where does the remark, "and to-morrow they Made Britain India," appear?
6. Who vows vengeance on a sailor because his wife refused to give her any of the chestnuts she was eating?

7. What Englishman, captured by the French, prefers death to being exchanged for an inferior?
8. Who are the Nevils?
9. According to an old saying, where do you begin if you want to win France?
10. Who would "break a thousand oaths to reign one year"?
11. Does Mistress Quickly have any children?
12. Who has often blushed when acknowledging his illegitimate son?
13. What Prince complains that all the other nations think his country is full of drunkards?
14. Who says "it were an easy leap, To pluck bright honour from the pale-faced moon"?
15. Which Queen has learned how to make perfumes, distil and preserve so efficiently that even the King is impressed?
16. Who tries to quiet rebels by telling them a tale of how "all the body's members Rebell'd against the belly"?
17. Name the merchant who tells the story of his life to his captor.
18. Who, on learning of the death of his enemy, remarks that the news "should make a greater crack"?
19. What does "the toad, ugly and venomous" wear in his head?
20. Who would rather have a fool to make her merry than experience to make her sad?

3. "SUNDRY CONTEMPLATIONS"

1. Who says, "leave her to heaven," and who is meant by "her"?
2. What great conqueror is said to have done his heroic deeds

to please his mother rather than for the good of his country?

3. What brother and sister have names exactly alike except for the last letter or two?

4. What bride and groom speak different languages and require an interpreter?

5. What woman urges a young girl to commit bigamy?

6. "If it be a sin to covet honour," who is "the most offending soul alive"?

7. Who wishes the College of Cardinals would choose her husband for Pope and carry him to Rome?

8. Which bishop is accused of going to church only to pray against his enemies?

9. What girl's last words are, "Confusion fall," before she is deprived of her power of speech forever?

10. Who looks at his hands and says, "This is a sorry sight"?

11. Which play never changes scenes?

12. Who hopes that after he is married he and his wife will learn to love each other, and "upon familiarity will grow more contempt"?

13. What character is to be carved "as a dish fit for the gods"?

14. Who is "Done to death by slanderous tongues"?

15. What discouraged man decides to sell his land instead of drowning himself?

16. Who, during his own wedding ceremony, smacks the priest so hard he (the priest) falls over?

17. What rascal knows, as soon as he looks at a lady, that he has lost a wager but, like the villain he is, collects it anyway?

18. Name the boy who takes all the blame and punishment for the misdemeanors of his dog?

19. Who walks up and down the battlefield asking for himself?

20. During which comedy does one of the characters say, "If this were play'd upon a stage now, I could condemn it as an improbable fiction"?

4. "SUNDRY CONTEMPLATIONS"

1. Who "doth bestride the narrow world Like a Colossus"?
2. Whose "legs bestrid the ocean"?
3. What character says he may turn pale with anger, sickness, or hunger but not with love?
4. Who is best pleased by those things, "That befal preposterously"?
5. What talkative man "speaks an infinite deal of nothing, more than any man in all Venice"?
6. In which play does England have four kings?
7. Name the woman who threatens to "exhibit a bill in parliament for the putting down of men."
8. What King has men put to death who cannot answer a riddle and paradoxically orders one killed because he can?
9. This villain confesses, among other heinous acts, that he often "digg'd up dead men from their graves And set them upright at their dear friends' doors." Who is he?
10. Identify Brach Merriman, Clowder, Silver, Belman and Echo.
11. Who wishes he were a glove?
12. Name Andromache's father-in-law.
13. In which play is the heroine the only human female character?
14. Who vows to leave all "Taffeta phrases, silken terms precise," and "Three-pil'd hyperboles" out of his future love-making?
15. What character is so sure of his Queen's honesty that he

swears if she prove otherwise, to transform his wife's
boudoir into a stable and have his three young daughters
sterilized?

16. Who disguises himself as a bearded minister to talk to
a man who cannot see him?

17. What picturesque hero was once sold into slavery?

18. Who are the residents of Sandal Castle?

19. What young man is forced to leave home because his
wicked brother plans to burn his lodging when he is asleep
in it?

20. A King of France tells his lords to beware the girls of
a certain country. What country is it?

5. "SUNDRY CONTEMPLATIONS"

1. Name the patrician who is continually accused of not
loving the common people.

2. What nobleman does a King accuse of loving the common
people too much?

3. A Roman Emperor fears this rebel because the common
people love him too much. Name the rebel.

4. What Duke loves the people, but dislikes appearing before them or hearing their loud applause and saluta-
tions?

5. Identify, "The riot of the tipsy Bacchanals, Tearing the
Thracian singer in their rage."

6. What Queen requests her attendant to give her mandragora to drink so she can sleep away the time her lover
is gone?

7. How do we know Shakespeare was familiar with Rabelais?

8. Which of the plays is the shortest?

9. What does borrowing dull the edge of?

10. Falstaff has an "incurable disease" which he declares borrowing prolongs. What does he call this disease?
11. Who is so well read that he can "reason against reading"?
12. Identify the most famous gate-crasher.
13. Whose sword is decorated with "five flower-de-luces on each side"?
14. King Pharamond was the founder of what law?
15. Who says farewell to all his "greatness"?
16. Who says farewell to "Pride, pomp and circumstance"?
17. What is defined as "a fool, that makes us scan The outward habit by the inward man"?
18. Who, in farewell admonitions to her son, instructs him to be "check'd for silence, But never tax'd for speech"?
19. What two groups of people bite their thumbs at each other to show their hatred?
20. Where is the only instance of a page turned down in a book?

6. "SUNDRY CONTEMPLATIONS"

1. Who says, "Cry 'havoc!' kings"?
2. Who says, "Cry 'Havoc,' and let slip the dogs of war"?
3. Who says, "Do not cry havoc"?
4. What King wishes two duelists well when they meet at Coventry, and stops the duel before it starts?
5. Who, after twenty years of living in a cave with two kidnapped Princes, decides "The game is up"?
6. Which of the Ten Commandments did the "sanctimonious pirate" have scraped from the tablet he took to sea with him?
7. Who calls his own murder "foul and most unnatural"?
8. Name the only character who speaks English with an Irish accent.

9. Whose dying words are, "I kiss'd thee ere I kill'd thee: no way but this, Killing myself, to die upon a kiss"?

10. What Duke asks his murderers to be as cruel as possible so his death will not be forgotten?

11. What event takes place in Tours, in the presence of the Kings of France and Sicil, four Dukes, "seven earls, twelve barons and twenty bishops"?

12. Which Queen refers to her youth as her "salad days" when she was "green in judgment"?

13. In the quotation, "no man's pie is freed From his ambitious finger," whose finger is it?

14. Who has been "an unlawful bawd" but is willing to be "a lawful hangman"?

15. What impecunious man admits he wants to marry a woman for her money?

16. What man, wealthy in his own right, is willing to marry a woman as "old as Sibyl" and as "shrewd as Socrates' Xantippe," just so she is rich?

17. Who "would fain die a dry death"?

18. Which character "few things loves better Than to abhor himself"?

19. Who is willing to risk his "three drops of blood" to defend the beauty and chastity of his lady?

20. What group lives "like the old Robin Hood of England"?

7. "SUNDRY CONTEMPLATIONS"

1. Name the girl who tears up her sweetheart's letter and then kisses each of the pieces.

2. Whose voice is "ear-deafening" and "Kin to Jove's thunder"?

3. Who is credited with establishing the institutions of learning at Ipswich and Oxford?

4. Name the Roman bride who begs another woman to kill her.

5. Identify the two Kings who are married to their brothers' widows.

6. Who turns his older brothers against each other so he can have everything his own way?

7. Which Queen of England appears in four plays?

8. Who "does smile his face into more lines than is in the new map with the augmentation of the Indies"?

9. What was "caviare to the general"?

10. Between what two characters is there a continual "skirmish of wit"?

11. What father is especially shocked at his daughter's behavior because she had always been "A maiden never bold; Of spirit so still and quiet that her motion Blush'd at herself"?

12. Identify the couple who quarrel so bitterly over a little Indian boy that their frightened followers hide in acorn cups.

13. What King deliberately keeps his daughter unmarried?

14. Who is accused of drinking himself out of "his five sentences"?

15. Whose mind is "tossing on the ocean"?

16. Identify the following: Master Rash, Master Caper, Dizy, Master Deep-vow, Master Copper-spur, Master Starve-lackey, and Drop-heir.

17. What beloved national hero easily usurps the throne while the lawful heir is out of the country?

18. Give the answer to the riddle: "What was a month old at Cain's birth, that's not five weeks old yet"?

19. Name the two characters who harp on the number of men in their father's retinue when they are trying to get rid of him.
20. Which soldiers have "ladies' faces and fierce dragons' spleens"?

8. "SUNDRY CONTEMPLATIONS"

1. What young man swears before the priest, who officiates at his wedding, that he will not consummate the marriage?
2. Who thinks that "Seven hundred pounds and possibilities is goot gifts" for a bride to bring?
3. Which play has the longest word, the longest scene, and the longest act?
4. Whose wound that was like a T has become an H?
5. Who is the only stepmother, appearing as such, in any of the plays?
6. What two girls are inseparable as Juno's swans, and have been since childhood?
7. Whose ghost vanishes at the crow of a cock?
8. Who is the brother of Lady Percy?
9. Where do the Wars of the Roses actually begin?
10. Name the widow who refuses to be a King's mistress and becomes his Queen.
11. Who helps murder a man he once saved from drowning?
12. Identify the rebel who promises England "seven halfpenny loaves" for a penny, and ten hoops for "the three-hooped pot."
13. Who uses the terms Flibbertigibbet, Smulkin, Modo, Obidicut and Hobbididence?
14. Who has a penthouse attached to his dwelling?
15. How should you speak "if you speak love"?

16. Who used a sword to woo a lady and won her?
17. What is made of silk that "hallow'd" worms did breed?
18. Identify: Dardan, Timbria, Helias, Chetas, Troien and Antenorides.
19. Does Tybalt, Bertram, or the Duke of Bedford say, "unbidden guests Are welcomest when they are gone"?
20. In which play is the Trojan Horse mentioned?

9. "SUNDRY CONTEMPLATIONS"

1. What four characters were born in Epidamnum?
2. Who boasts to her companions that she has a "pilot's thumb"?
3. What young man finances his trip to Italy with the dowry the King of France gives his bride?
4. "Consideration like an angel came And whipp'd the offending Adam out of" whom?
5. Who would rather not live than be in awe of himself?
6. How much time elapses between the end of "Richard II" and the beginning of "Henry IV, Part I"?
7. In which play does a cobbler lead men about the streets so they will wear out their shoes and give him more work?
8. Who is the grandmother of Prince Arthur?
9. Who blames the treachery between parents and children on the recent eclipses of the sun and moon?
10. What kind of fish are in both the river in Macedon and the one at Monmouth?
11. Who "was ever precise in promise-keeping" and is already two hours late for an appointment?
12. Identify "Lady Disdain" who would rather hear her dog bark at a crow than a man swear he loves her.

13. Who ventures the opinion, "The course of true love never did run smooth"?
14. Which girl named Anne has a brother named William?
15. Who has received "fair speechless messages" from a lady's eyes?
16. Name the eighty-year-old man who gives his young master all of his savings, and follows him into exile.
17. What other Brutus besides Marcus and Decius join in the betrayal of a great Roman?
18. What is defined as "a pipe Blown by surmises, jealousies, conjectures"?
19. Who uses the word, "honorificabilitudinitatibus"?
20. Who says, "Something is rotten in the state of Denmark"?

10. "SUNDRY CONTEMPLATIONS"

1. Who is accused by his daughter of showing a "tender fatherly regard" in wishing to marry her to a "half-lunatic"?
2. Identify the young man who thinks he can "fast, being loose" rather than in prison, and he can also fast better on a full stomach.
3. What Queen threatens to corrupt her daughter's manners, disfigure her, and prove her illegitimate to save her from an habitual murderer, and then agrees to let her marry him?
4. Name the dying man who speaks lovingly of England as "This royal throne of kings, this scepter'd isle," and so on.
5. From what country do the kernes and gallowglasses come?
6. Who says, "I will wear my heart upon my sleeve For daws to peck at"?
7. What conqueror bares his throat to be cut and swoons,

because the people show they do not want him for their king?

8. Who presents his throat to a man and tells him he would be a fool not to cut it?

9. Identify "the pretty worm of Nilus there, That kills and pains not."

10. Who is "a snapper-up of unconsidered trifles"?

11. Which play has the alternate title, "What You Will"?

12. Does Valentine, Benedick, or Parolles say, "A young man married is a man that's marr'd"?

13. What brave soldier is said to fight like a thousand men?

14. In order to save the life of his illegitimate infant, this man turns informer against the mother of the child and her sons. Name him.

15. What pair is married at the Pantheon in Rome?

16. Who gives an elaborate banquet at which precious stones are presented as favors?

17. Name the girl who proposes to a young man she has known only an hour or so by saying, "I am your wife, if you will marry me."

18. The action of which play takes place eleven years after an earthquake?

19. Who calls his stepfather "A king of shreds and patches," among other things.

20. Who is given gold to poison a prince, but is forbidden to ask the reason why?

11. "SUNDRY CONTEMPLATIONS"

1. What young lady swears she would not be Queen for "all the riches under heaven," but becomes one anyway?

2. Who is father-in-law to both Prince Edward and the Duke of Clarence?

3. What character "reads much," "loves no plays," "hears no music," and "seldom smiles"?

4. Who lies "in a cowslip's bell," and flies "on the bat's back"?

5. Who agrees to marry the daughter of the Earl of Armagnac and then jilts her?

6. What happened to the man who sold the lion's skin while the lion was still alive?

7. During what interval does Mistress Quickly become "a poor widow of Eastcheap"?

8. Name the King of England who envies one of his subjects whose son he considers superior to his own Prince of Wales.

9. Who threatens to make a ghost of anyone who tries to stop him from following a ghost?

10. In what city are a Briton, an Italian, a Dutchman, a Frenchman, and a Spaniard present at a discussion on the honesty of women?

11. This Roman General is willing to "lean upon one crutch, and fight with t'other" rather than stay out of the war. Who is he?

12. Which pair of sisters has neither a mother nor a father appearing with them?

13. Who tells a King to his face that his majesty is "borrowed"?

14. What Roman, when his behavior is being questioned, asks "What was 't to you?"

15. Who successfully imitates his half-brother's handwriting?

16. What Duke has a wrestler of his own?

17. Who are addressed as "imperfect speakers"?

18. What mother is temporarily so embittered against her son, she moans, "I do wash his name out of my blood"?

19. Who, on the day she is to take her vows as a nun, meets with circumstances that lead her to recant and take a husband?
20. In which play are a Princess and her attendants required to live in tents?

12. "SUNDRY CONTEMPLATIONS"

1. What relation is the Marquis of Dorset to Edward IV?
2. Which pair of sisters has a father but no mother appearing with them?
3. Which play ends with a triple wedding?
4. Name the only character in any of the plays who has written a book to be published.
5. Name the two brothers who are opposing candidates for the throne of Rome.
6. What Prince lives in his father's palace with another man's wife?
7. In which play do three males wear feminine clothes?
8. Who tells a story of having shot a second arrow in order to find the first one, to justify his own procedure?
9. Give the six words that follow, "What's Hecuba to him, or he to Hecuba."
10. Where is there a famine so drastic that some of the otherwise civilized citizens are ready to become cannibals?
11. Who says repeatedly, "Put money in thy purse," and to whom does he say it?
12. Which King is accused of spending more in peace than his ancestors did in wars?
13. What young man considers marrying a milkmaid who "hath more qualities than a water-spaniel," "more wealth than faults," and talks in her sleep?

14. Which King orders one of his lords to poison another King who is a guest in his house?
15. Who makes a great noise about losing his drum?
16. Name the Queen whose "person, It beggar'd all description."
17. Who is speaking and who is referred to in the following quotation: "Was ever woman in this humour woo'd? Was ever woman in this humour won?"
18. Which play begins with a sonnet?
19. Who, "being transported And rapt in secret studies," let his dukedom get away from him?
20. Who is "by birth a pedlar, by education a card-maker, by transmutation a bear-herd, and now by present profession a tinker"?

13. "SUNDRY CONTEMPLATIONS"

1. In whom "appears The constant service of the antique world"?
2. What man challenges a young girl to a duel and loses it?
3. Who laments, "My shame will not be shifted with my sheet"?
4. What is the title of the father and son who are beheaded in *Richard III* and *Henry VIII*, respectively, both betrayed by their servants?
5. Who says, "lend me your ears"?
6. Who says, "Lend me your knees"?
7. Who asks a man to lend his ear and then strikes him on it?
8. What mother knows her son is not entitled to the crown, but fights for him to keep it anyway?
9. Who says she is going for a sail "in a sieve"?
10. What is it "greasy Joan doth keel"?

11. Where is there "Not a mouse stirring"?
12. Identify the "Weed" that is so lovely and "smell'st so sweet."
13. Name the villain who has himself delivered to a lady's bedroom in a trunk.
14. Who has been traveling around for seven years looking for his brother and mother?
15. What simple young man is discovered hiding in a closet in a French doctor's house?
16. Who admires his enemy so much that if he were not himself he would want to be that enemy?
17. What dying nobleman admits that he deserves no pity at the hands of his enemies?
18. Which play is the longest?
19. Give the famous six words that follow, "When you shall these unlucky deeds relate."
20. What man, feigning death, overhears his friend's grief at losing him?

14. "SUNDRY CONTEMPLATIONS"

1. Who thinks he "could deal kingdoms" to his friends "and ne'er be weary"?
2. Whose suitors come from Italy, England, Germany, France, Morocco and "Arragon"?
3. Name the Princess on whose birthday "there are princes and knights come from all parts of the world to just and tourney for her love."
4. What Queen is taken captive and then made Empress of her conquerors?
5. What young girl is listening to a story so shocking that when she is asked, "Dost thou hear?" she replies, "Your tale, sir, would cure deafness"?

6. Which Queen is falsely accused of plotting her husband's death?
7. Who is "valiant as the lion, churlish as the bear, slow as the elephant"?
8. What bridegroom, immediately after his wedding, orders his bride to go home to his mother?
9. What is "the most unkindest cut of all"?
10. Which follower of Falstaff appears in four plays?
11. Who has for his entertainment the singing of twenty nightingales and is promised a couch softer than the one contrived for Semiramis?
12. Whose dying words are, "Di faciant laudis summa sit ista tuae!"?
13. What King and Queen accuse each other of having had an affair with a betrothed woman and man, respectively?
14. Who cannot believe "for a season after" he awakes from a nightmare that he is not in hell?
15. What man is almost annihilated by two women he meets at a venison dinner?
16. Whose chariot is "an empty hazel-nut"?
17. The battle of Dunsinane ends which play?
18. Who is held up by a pair of outlaws and, for reasons of his own, becomes one of them?
19. What do the lunatic, the lover and the poet have in common?
20. Who tells his dying uncle that he is a "lunatic lean-witted fool"?

15. "SUNDRY CONTEMPLATIONS"

1. Who has been "rated" many times in the Rialto?
2. In which play does the only nun appear?

3. Who stabs himself in the arm to make his father think his half-brother is a villain?
4. What house guest sends a diamond with greetings to "a most kind hostess"?
5. Who trusts his servant with his gold and beats the servant's brother for not having it?
6. By what "sin fell the angels"?
7. Who, when discussing an illiterate man says, "he hath not eat paper, as it were; he hath not drunk ink"?
8. What French King hopes for the fall of an English King "For mocking marriage with a dame of France"?
9. Who is deprived of a substantial inheritance because his half-brother proves him illegitimate?
10. Name the English Kings who belong to the House of York.
11. What is it "whose tongue Outvenoms all the worms of the Nile; whose breath Rides on the posting winds, and doth belie All corners of the world"?
12. Who gives a long discourse on the advantages of drinking sherris-sack?
13. The title of what play within a play is changed to "The Mouse Trap"?
14. Who obeys a King's orders to stick a glove in his cap and thereby receives a box on his ear and a glove full of money?
15. Name the great character who greets his untalkative wife with "My gracious silence."
16. Who refuses to surrender the war prisoners he has captured because the King refuses to ransom the man's brother-in-law?
17. Identify the girl who exclaims, "O wonderful, wonderful, and most wonderful wonderful! and yet again wonderful!"
18. Who suggests playing a game of billiards?
19. This captured soldier is exhibited in an open market-place

as a public spectacle with scoffs, scorns and taunts. Name him.

20. Who, during a violent thunderstorm, goes about in it with his "bosom" bared, tempting the lightning to strike him?

16. "SUNDRY CONTEMPLATIONS"

1. Name the woman who became a kidnapper and was rewarded with a husband.
2. If sorrows "come not single spies," how do they come?
3. This woman, if she had been the wife of Hercules, would have done "six of his labours" and saved her husband "so much sweat."
4. Who is "the fairies' midwife"?
5. What hired murderer sincerely regrets his bargain, refuses to do any of the stabbing, or take any of the fee?
6. Who brags that he once wrote music to English ditties for the harp and sang them?
7. "From the crown of his head to the sole of his foot, he is all mirth." Who is he?
8. Who accuses his new son-in-law of practicing "foul charms"?
9. Who accuses his future son-in-law of winning his daughter with "rings, gawds, conceits, Knacks, trifles, nosegays," and so on?
10. Who feels like crying right in the middle of a song he is singing?
11. What character is willing to buy, sell, talk and walk with his enemies, but not eat, drink nor pray with them?
12. Name the young man who is made an example of because

he violates a statute that has been ignored for fourteen years.

13. What couple is living at Inverness when their story begins?
14. Who "draweth out the thread of his verbosity finer than the staple of his argument"?
15. For whose hand are the King of France and the Duke of Burgundy rival suitors?
16. In whose speech do the following expressions appear: "to paint the lily, To throw a perfume on the violet, To smooth the ice, or add another hue Unto the rainbow"?
17. " 'Tis common proof" that what is "young ambition's ladder"?
18. What churchman amasses great wealth for the purpose of paying his way into the Pope's chair?
19. Who seems to be Falstaff's favorite girl?
20. Which King of England is the son of Edward, the Black Prince?

17. "SUNDRY CONTEMPLATIONS"

1. Name the only character who mentions America.
2. Whose job is to "wash, wring, brew, bake, scour, dress meat and drink, make the beds" and do it all herself?
3. Whose last words are, "Thus with a kiss I die"?
4. What two brothers are willing to kill each other over a married woman who scarcely knows they are alive?
5. Who exits, "pursued by a bear"?
6. In the line, "The earth hath bubbles as the water has," what are the "bubbles"?
7. What is the occasion for the comment, "there is nothing either good or bad, but thinking makes it so"?

8. What "Plays such fantastic tricks before high heaven As make the angels weep"?

9. Who, having no mail box, posts his love notes on trees?

10. What fifteen-year-old girl, unable to remember how she cried when she was a child, says she "Will cry it o'er again"?

11. Who is so irritated with a talkative man that he asks him to speak in a foreign language so he cannot understand what he is saying?

12. Who is the talkative man?

13. Name the two army officers who loll in their tent during a war, ridiculing their superiors.

14. Who, after being stabbed, is drowned in a "malmsey-butt"?

15. Whose nature is so honest and frank "He would not flatter Neptune for his trident, Or Jove for 's power to thunder"?

16. What King is willing to relinquish his crown, but wants to keep his griefs as his own?

17. A fire from heaven shrivelled up what two characters?

18. Who has "very poor and unhappy brains for drinking"?

19. Which Duke has a Master of Revels in his court?

20. Who helps his friend win a girl by impersonating him at a masked ball?

18. "SUNDRY CONTEMPLATIONS"

1. What woman faints when she is told three murders have been committed instead of one?

2. Who tells the man she mistakes for her husband that once her words were music to his ear?

3. What Roman gains great sea power by making an alliance with a pair of pirates?
4. Name the constable who orders a member of his guard to "comprehend all vagrom men."
5. What great character speaks almost exclusively in prose through three plays?
6. This nephew of a King fights on the side of the enemy. Name him.
7. Who complains that his heart has turned to stone and it hurts his hand to strike it?
8. What young Queen deplores her position and would rather be dead than hear men say, "God save the Queen!"?
9. This girl steals money and jewelry from her father, and her friends seem to approve of it. Who is she?
10. Who is presented with a portrait of himself by the artist?
11. What, "like a worm i' the bud," fed "on her damask cheek"?
12. Name the man whose doctrine on the transmigration of souls is mentioned in three plays.
13. What woman's only fault is "that she is intolerable curst"?
14. Who becomes a wealthy man by a merciful deed?
15. What murdered man is reported to have died from the sting of a serpent?
16. Who marries the daughter of the man who captured him and is considered a traitor for doing so?
17. What French city is lost by the English and won again the same day?
18. Who makes the logical deduction that since it is ten o'clock, it was nine an hour ago, and will be eleven an hour from now?
19. What church dignitary is tried for heretical teachings?
20. Who is only joking when he says he would rather be a pedlar than King of England?

19. "SUNDRY CONTEMPLATIONS"

1. What ambitious lady is ensnared in a trap when she is called "your royal majesty" by a crafty priest?
2. Identify the priest.
3. What is "oft led by the nose with gold"?
4. Which hero attended school in Wittenburg?
5. Name the three characters who carry on Falstaff's penchant for thievery after his death.
6. Whose ancestors drove Tarquin from the streets of Rome?
7. Which King takes his mother and niece to France with him when he goes to fight a war?
8. Where does "Veni, vidi, vici" appear?
9. At whose birth did "The frame and huge foundation of the earth" shake "like a coward"?
10. What child once tore a butterfly to pieces?
11. Name the two bickering men who are the instigators of the Wars of the Roses.
12. What "knits up the ravell'd sleeve of care"?
13. In whose fireplace are silver andirons made in the form of "two winking Cupids" each standing on one foot?
14. Who wants to marry a simple country girl until he sees the ladies of the French court?
15. What man contends that he did not receive a large amount of money which his debtor claims to have sent him on account?
16. Who kills himself rather than obey his friend's orders to kill *him?*
17. In which play do three females dress as males?
18. Who thinks that her husband will be a better man for having been a little bad?

19. What young lady claims she was an Irish rat in another incarnation but does not remember it very well?

20. What King is continually addressed as "nuncle" by his jester?

20. "SUNDRY CONTEMPLATIONS"

1. Who blesses the bees that made the wax her husband's letter is sealed with?

2. Whose speech begins: "Romans, friends, followers, favourers of my right"?

3. Identify the two duelists who wait in different locations for each other, and then together vow vengeance on the arrangers who play the joke on them.

4. Who is exhorted to "look like the innocent flower, But be the serpent under 't"?

5. Does Brutus or Macbeth say: "Between the acting of a dreadful thing And the first motion, all the interim is Like a phantasma or a hideous dream"?

6. Who was once knighted by Richard Coeur-de-Lion?

7. Who says "Measure for measure must be answered"?

8. Under what condition does a young man say, "It is a wise father that knows his own child"?

9. Of the large assortment of French men and women in the plays, which are the only ones who speak English with a French accent?

10. Name the hysterical Princess who goes around inciting her countrymen to "Cry!"

11. In which play does one male, only, dress as a female?

12. Who orders the loud sounds of trumpets and drums so he cannot hear what his mother and sister-in-law are saying?

13. What baby is born aboard ship in a raging storm?
14. Who says, "How sharper than a serpent's tooth it is To have a thankless child!"?
15. Who is the "thankless child" referred to?
16. When Cupid's bolt fell on a milk-white flower, what color did the flower change to?
17. Who made "such a sinner of his memory To credit his own lie," he really believed he was the Duke of Milan?
18. Name the schoolmaster who gives his opinion on the pronunciation of such words as debt, calf, half and neigh.
19. Whose favorite cliché is, "That is the humour of it," and its variations?
20. Who tells of encountering men in his travels "whose heads Do grow beneath their shoulders"?

21. "SUNDRY CONTEMPLATIONS"

1. Who, in his last dying words, prays that his murderer be forgiven?
2. "Tear-falling pity dwells not" in whose eye?
3. Name the conjurer who diagnoses the cases of two characters by their "pale and deadly looks."
4. Who was the "fellow of infinite jest"?
5. Who frightens a serpent away, kills a lioness, and saves his brother's life?
6. What man steps out of his hiding place to "whip hypocrisy"?
7. Whose horses go wild and "eat each other"?
8. What name is used frequently to designate any rustic or servant girl?
9. Which of the girls who don male attire is ashamed of her appearance?

10. What character deliberately arranges for his wife to fall in love with another man?

11. Having fallen from the heights, this man finds the "blessedness of being little." Name him.

12. What other man besides Julius Caesar is said to have epileptic fits?

13. Who hides a bag of gold under an elder-tree to be used in a murderous plot?

14. Believing her husband lost forever, this woman takes her vows as a vestal in the Temple of Diana at Ephesus. Who is she?

15. Who is himself when he is alone, but in all other places he is his master?

16. Who is warned in a letter, which he never reads, to look about him if he is not immortal?

17. Who writes this letter?

18. What is "very apoplexy, lethargy, mull'd, deaf, sleepy, insensible; a getter of more bastard children than war's a destroyer of men"?

19. Who says who is "the courageous captain of compliments"?

20. What do both Rosalind and Cymbeline's Queen call Caesar's "came, saw and overcame"?

22. "SUNDRY CONTEMPLATIONS"

1. What is made of sighs, tears, wishes, adoration, duty, patience, impatience and numerous other qualities?

2. Who tells his persistent wife that what she does not know, she cannot tell, and that is as far as he will trust her?

3. Who slips into a brook and drowns while hanging "fantastic garlands" on a willow tree?

4. Name the Earl who accuses his innocent son of treachery.
5. Who sleeps well "after life's fitful fever"?
6. What are the given names of the two Princes who are murdered in the Tower?
7. Who are the father and mother of these two Princes?
8. What did "the old hermit of Prague, that never saw pen and ink, very wittily" say to the niece of King Gorboduc?
9. Who says, "Comparisons are odorous"?
10. In the quotation, "a lion among ladies is a most dreadful thing," is the word "lion" used figuratively or does it really mean an animal?
11. What man complains that he has a "kind of alacrity in sinking"?
12. Who is a confessed braggart when he tells his bride that all the wealth he has runs in his veins?
13. What bird "on every tree, mocks married men"?
14. Name the usurping King who insists the murder of the real heir to the throne had not entered his mind until he looked at a disfigured man "fit for bloody villainy."
15. Who is this disfigured man?
16. Which woman wounds her own thigh to show herself what she can endure better than her husband's silence?
17. What "acquaints a man with strange bedfellows"?
18. Identify the only stepbrother and stepsister combination.
19. Who uses the expression, "multitudinous seas incarnadine"?
20. What girl tells a young man when he first kisses her that he kisses "by the book"?

23. "SUNDRY CONTEMPLATIONS"

1. Who "jests at scars that never felt a wound"?
2. Which father has a trio of daughters?

3. Who calls the Tower of London "Julius Caesar's ill-erected tower"?
4. Which character delivers the longest soliloquy?
5. Who deceivingly bets on a man to win a duel when he knows he will be killed?
6. What pair "no sooner met but they looked; no sooner looked but they loved; no sooner loved but they sighed"?
7. Who thanks God that he is "as honest as any man living that is an old man and no honester" than he?
8. Which King knows "no way to mince it in love, but directly to say 'I love you' "?
9. "Who steals my purse," steals what?
10. In whose business affairs do Tripolis, Mexico, England, Lisbon, Barbary and India figure?
11. What reeks with "the rankest compound of villanous smell that ever offended nostril"?
12. Who says, "Thersites' body is as good as Ajax', When neither are alive"?
13. How many characters speak English with a Welsh accent?
14. Which Duke thinks that since he can "add colours to the chameleon, Change shapes with Proteus for advantages, And set the murderous Machiavel to school," he should be able to get the crown of England?
15. What other woman, besides Lady Macbeth, tries to entice her husband to usurp a throne?
16. Whose slashed mantle is exhibited at his funeral?
17. This man, when he impersonates a King, speaks "in King Cambyses' vein." Who is he?
18. Who has "all the royal makings of a queen" and is crowned with "Edward Confessor's crown"?
19. Name the King who sings when he is dying.
20. Which fairy thinks that mortals are fools?

24. "SUNDRY CONTEMPLATIONS"

1. Who "loves to hear himself talk, and will speak more in a minute than he will stand to in a month"?
2. What son leads his blind father to believe he has fallen from a great height and lived through it?
3. Name the "pearl, Whose price hath launch'd above a thousand ships."
4. What does "the whirligig of time" bring?
5. Who, in a song, "excels each mortal thing Upon the dull earth dwelling"?
6. Identify the group of men who disguise themselves as Russians to play a prank.
7. Who is the only native Russian in any of the plays?
8. Whose ghost appears three times and says nothing?
9. For what reason is the song rendered that begins, "Tell me where is fancy bred"?
10. Who is willing to give "a thousand furlongs of sea for an acre of barren ground"?
11. Who is warned by his mother that if he were to give his grandmother a kingdom, his grandam would give him "a plum, a cherry and a fig"?
12. The famous speeches of what two men are made at the Forum in Rome?
13. Ipswich is the birthplace of what gentleman of the cloth?
14. Which Queen raises an army of thirty thousand men to attack a traitor to the King?
15. Who (a) calls whom (b) "Mephostophilus"?
16. Who says, "A horse! a horse! my kingdom for a horse!"?
17. Who says, "O, for a horse with wings!"?

18. What is paradoxical about the remark: "brevity is the soul of wit"?
19. Who "uses his folly like a stalking-horse and under the presentation of that he shoots his wit"?
20. What Princess is "buxom, blithe and full of face"?

25. "SUNDRY CONTEMPLATIONS"

1. What wife is not allowed to taste the meat her husband prepares for her until she thanks him?
2. The action of which play covers only three hours?
3. Who threatens to select his heir from among the beggars of the world if his only daughter marries against his will?
4. Who says his wife is "a deadly theme" and asks that her name be not mentioned?
5. Which English King loves France so well he will not part with a village of it?
6. Who features singing commercials?
7. What woman drops dead right after she is kissed by another woman?
8. Who is being referred to in the line: "I never knew so young a body with so old a head"?
9. What is it that "all the perfumes of Arabia will not sweeten"?
10. Who tries to console a young man condemned to death by telling him that when you are old and rich you have "neither heat, affection, limb, nor beauty" to make your riches enjoyable?
11. What mother is less than thirty years old when her daughter gets married?
12. Name the two girls who once sat on the same cushion,

worked on the same sampler, warbled the same song in
the same key, and now fight over men.

13. What father grieves because his daughter "is fallen Into a
    pit of ink"?
14. In which play do two husbands kill their wives on stage?
15. Identify these husbands and wives.
16. Who is the only other man to murder his wife (this one
    poisons her off stage)?
17. What man's wife dies on stage from poison he intended
    for someone else?
18. Who examines his face in a mirror and calls it a "flatter-
    ing glass" because it does not show deeper wrinkles?
19. Who asks for a mirror to see if his daughter is breathing?
20. "Day, night, hour, tide, time," "Alone, in company,"
    whose chief care has been to find a husband for his
    daughter?

26. "SUNDRY CONTEMPLATIONS"

1. Who is "wedded to calamity"?
2. Where does the following familiar quotation appear:
   "some are born great, some achieve greatness, and some
   have greatness thrust upon 'em"?
3. In which play do three Queens of England appear?
4. Name these three Queens.
5. Who begins to suspect that he is being "fopped"?
6. Which character is given four whimsical creatures to
   attend his wants and "Feed him with apricocks, and dew-
   berries, With purple grapes, green figs, and mulberries"?
7. Name the wicked woman who writes a rhymed epitaph
   for an empty grave.
8. Who is given to "taverns, and sack, and wine, and me-

theglins, and to drinkings, and swearings, and starings, pribbles and prabbles"?
9. Where do we find the line, "All that glisters is not gold"?
10. Which of the many warriors says he is willing to fight "i' the air"?
11. Because of a quarrel with a servant, this disguised nobleman is put in stocks. What's his name?
12. Who delivers an eloquent dissertation on the subject of "Commodity"?
13. Who is the daughter of Cato?
14. What King vows to sleep sitting up, even in his tent, until either he or his enemy is vanquished?
15. Who calls whom a "fishmonger"?
16. Who has his beard singed off, huge buckets of mud thrown on him to put out the fire, and is nicked "like a fool"?
17. Who has a stepson named Demetrius?
18. Who thinks it is bitter "to look into happiness through another man's eyes"?
19. Identify the second century Greek physician who is mentioned in four plays.
20. What displaced Princess is "The queen of curds and cream"?

27. "SUNDRY CONTEMPLATIONS"

1. Does Caliban or Mercutio exclaim, "O flesh, flesh, how art thou fishified!"?
2. What Queen Dowager gloats over the misfortunes of her enemies?
3. Who hates a proud man but, the general opinion is, loves himself?
4. Having been made to believe his daughter is dead, this

father dons sackcloth and swears never to wash his face
or cut his hair.

5. What is it that "not poppy, nor mandragora, Nor all
the drowsy syrups of the world" can produce?

6. Whose "disgrace is to be called boy; but his glory is to
subdue men"?

7. What are "a few of the unpleasant'st words That ever
blotted paper"?

8. Who asks his companions to "laugh" him to sleep?

9. Which character is afraid a Welsh fairy is going to turn
him into a piece of cheese?

10. When did "Men, wives and children stare, cry out and run
As it were doomsday"?

11. What Prince dies when he falls from a prison wall?

12. This bride pays a woman and her daughter handsomely
to help her make a date with her own husband. Who is she?

13. What married man says of a girl he has captured: "She's
beautiful and therefore to be woo'd; She is a woman, therefore to be won"?

14. Who is the captured woman?

15. What former enemy has become so heroic to an army that
the soldiers "use him as grace 'fore meat, Their talk at table
and their thanks at end"?

16. Who was Cassibelan?

17. What two women are put in prison as accomplices in beating a man to death?

18. What entertainment is described as consisting of some ten
words, which is ten words too long, and not "one word
apt" nor one well cast player?

19. Who asks to be buried alive in the grave with his dead
sister?

20. Who owns a gray horse called Capilet?

28. "SUNDRY CONTEMPLATIONS"

1. Who is "More sinn'd against than sinning"?
2. What distraught hostess orders her dinner guests to leave at once and disregard formalities?
3. Who loaned his Book of Riddles to Alice Shortcake on All-hallowmas?
4. What is the longest single personal name?
5. Who "threw a pearl away Richer than all his tribe"?
6. In what city is the annual feast of Neptune celebrated?
7. Who appears to hang "upon the cheek of night Like a rich jewel in an Ethiop's ear"?
8. What dethroned King helps put his crown on his successor's head?
9. Whose ship is wrecked by a storm in "the still-vex'd Bermoothes"?
10. Who is obviously convinced that he has been sleeping for fifteen years?
11. What impoverished nobleman digs in the ground for roots to eat and finds only gold, which he cannot eat?
12. Who, feeling he cannot be a lover, is determined to be a villain?
13. Identify the mother who orders her new-born baby killed.
14. Name the patrician who "loves a cup of hot wine with not a drop of allaying Tiber in 't."
15. Who, of his own volition, leaves a comfortable home to become a traitor and live uncomfortably among strangers in an army camp?
16. What pair lives "in the skirts of the forest, like fringe upon a petticoat"?

17. Who is "snatch'd one half out of the jaws of death"?
18. Who snatched him?
19. What indignant father locks his daughter in a tower every night to keep her from eloping?
20. What Frenchman is made a general in an Italian army?

29. "SUNDRY CONTEMPLATIONS"

1. What young lady loves her husband so much she wants to be a soldier and follow him into battle?
2. Name the two tribunes who are put to death for removing the trophies of a hero from the streets of Rome.
3. Whose name is given as "Richard du Champ" after he is dead?
4. This dying man's heart is "fracted and corroborate." Who is he?
5. The announcement of what news is accompanied with "trumpets, sackbuts, psalteries and fifes, Tabors and cymbals," and shouts?
6. What rascal, blindfolded by his comrades, thinks he is giving military secrets to the enemy?
7. What, in man or woman, is "the immediate jewel of their souls"?
8. Name the go-between in several mischievous intrigues who is called "she-Mercury."
9. Who bears a "duke's revenues on her back," and scorns the poverty of the Queen, according to the Queen?
10. What "proclaims the man" that should be "rich, not gaudy"?
11. Which King resigns the government of his country to two men he considers worthy, so he can live a simple and prayerful life?

12. Name these two trusted men.
13. At whose tomb do Pyramus and Thisbe plan to meet?
14. Which character, besides the ronyon in Macbeth, uses the expression, "aroint thee, witch"?
15. Who is Diana Capilet?
16. Name the two men who meet the first time in the wilds of Gloucestershire, become devoted allies, and later bitter enemies.
17. Who is found under a tree in the forest, "like a dropped acorn" or "a wounded knight"?
18. What are they "that can count their worth"?
19. Who hires teachers of music, mathematics, and languages for his daughters?
20. Where do we find the lines, "Some there be that shadows kiss; Such have but a shadow's bliss"?

30. "SUNDRY CONTEMPLATIONS"

1. What English soldier dies in France holding his newly slain son in his arms?
2. Who, for twelve years, was kept prisoner in a pine rift?
3. Identify the three members of the Minola family.
4. Who, during a street fight, is wounded and bewails: "A plague o' both your houses"?
5. What Bishop is sent for the good strawberries growing in his garden when his absence is desired?
6. What nobleman is put to death by an outlaw because he "traitorously corrupted the youth of the realm in erecting a grammar school" and a paper mill, caused printing to be used, and speaks Latin and French?
7. Who is the grandfather of Marina?
8. Who is Sweno?

9. What lone villain does everyone trust and no one suspect until the end?

10. Identify the young boy who is given a lesson in Latin on the street by a Welshman.

11. What "becomes The throned monarch better than his crown"?

12. In which play does Mistress Quickly die "i' the spital"?

13. Who makes the longest uninterrupted speech?

14. Who makes the longest interrupted speech?

15. What "bubble" does the soldier seek, "Even in the cannon's mouth"?

16. Whose speech contains the advice: "to thine own self be true"?

17. Identify Lady Percy's mother-in-law.

18. Which character delivers the greatest number of soliloquies?

19. Name the woman whose dead body is ordered thrown to beasts and birds of prey.

20. Which future King of England was born with teeth, while the night-crow cried and the owl shrieked?

31. "SUNDRY CONTEMPLATIONS"

1. Which King is upbraided by his Queen because he will neither fight nor run?

2. Who is the man that "a lady in Venice would have walked barefoot to Palestine for a touch of his nether lip"?

3. Name the devoted wife who kills herself by swallowing fire.

4. What Duke is executed on All-Souls' day?

5. On whose brow is shame "ashamed to sit"?

6. Which city in Italy is the "nursery of arts"?

7. Who declares that he was not blown hither by "the ill wind which blows no man to good"?
8. Identify the expression, "miching mallecho."
9. What Briton joins the Italian army, changes his clothes when he gets to Britain, and fights against the Italians?
10. Name Virgilia's mother-in-law.
11. Which is the only play that does not call for music of any kind—not even a flourish?
12. In whose speech do the following expressions appear: "Retort Courteous," "Quip Modest," "Reply Churlish," and "Reproof Valiant"?
13. Which play has fifteen scenes in one act?
14. If the fault "is not in our stars," where is it?
15. Who suffers "a sea-change Into something rich and strange"?
16. Who writes and reads aloud "an extemporal epitaph on the death of the deer"?
17. What is the man fit for "that hath no music in himself, Nor is not moved with concords of sweet sounds"?
18. Who plays "on his prologue like a child on a recorder"?
19. Who says to his nephew: "Grace me no grace, nor uncle me no uncle: I am no traitor's uncle"?
20. Who is the nephew?

32. "SUNDRY CONTEMPLATIONS"

1. Which play has the greatest percentage of prose lines?
2. Who once wrote a sonnet to his horse?
3. What dead man has "silver skin" and "golden blood"?
4. What Archbishop is required to wait like "a lousy footboy" outside the Council-chamber door for half an hour?

5. What villain's last statement is that he will never say another word?

6. Who says, "Approach thou like the rugged Russian bear, The arm'd rhinoceros, or the Hyrcan tiger; Take any shape but that, and my firm nerves Shall never tremble"?

7. To whom are these lines addressed?

8. This girl hears her false lover say she is dead, to excuse his own inconstancy. Name her.

9. Who is sure "care's an enemy to life"?

10. What two Princes are considered by their brother to be like those men "whom Aristotle thought Unfit to hear moral philosophy"?

11. Where is "every thing advantageous to life" except the "means to live"?

12. What two women admit they will do anything for gold?

13. Who says "there's small choice in rotten apples"?

14. What is "such sweet sorrow"?

15. Who has a white horse named Surrey?

16. On what King's head do "rude misgovern'd hands from windows' tops" throw dust and rubbish?

17. What royal house comes to power in England the first time with the ascent of Henry IV?

18. Who is said to be most flattered when he is told that he hates flatterers?

19. What fleet is destroyed off the coast of Cyprus by a storm?

20. Who says he is "a tainted wether of the flock, Meetest for death"?

33. "SUNDRY CONTEMPLATIONS"

1. Whose contradictory words are, "Though I did wish him dead, I hate the murderer, love him murdered"?

2. Who is the murdered man referred to?
3. What globe-trotter lands at Tarsus with his infant daughter?
4. Who, while he is "Being entertained for a perfumer," hides behind an arras and overhears a marriage being arranged?
5. Whose marriage is it?
6. Whose wedding festivities hold sway for two weeks?
7. Does Hamlet, Claudio, or Imogen say, "Ay, but to die, and go we know not where; To lie in cold obstruction and to rot"?
8. What saintly Queen was "Oftener upon her knees than on her feet, Died every day she lived"?
9. On whose birthday is the battle of Philippi fought?
10. What woman tells her expensive husband-to-be that since he is "dear bought," she will love him "dear"?
11. In which play is the battle of St. Alban's fought?
12. What group of men present a pageant entitled, "The Nine Worthies"?
13. Identify the dying King who tells his heir to keep "giddy minds" busy with foreign quarrels.
14. In what battle are the odds of slain men ten thousand Frenchmen to twenty-nine Englishmen?
15. Name the two Princes who conduct a funeral in song for a dead Prince and a seemingly dead Princess.
16. What father sends his servant to Paris with orders to check on his son's behavior and reputation?
17. Name the woman who is told by her husband she is "not worth the dust which the rude wind Blows" in her face.
18. Which play ends with a quadruple wedding?
19. What is being referred to when a French lord says, "I am heartily sorry that he'll be glad of this"?
20. Who bemoans the fact that she may have to dance barefoot at her sister's wedding?

34. "SUNDRY CONTEMPLATIONS"

1. Who says, "O, blood, blood, blood!"?
2. Who says, "O horror, horror, horror!"?
3. Who says, "O day! O day! O day! O hateful day!"?
4. What three men sit around a table and decide who shall live and who shall die?
5. Which Queen lays aside her "mourning weeds," and is "ready to put armour on"?
6. Who calls marriage a "world-without-end bargain"?
7. What ghost is dressed "in his habit as he lived"?
8. Whose dying words are, "The drink, the drink! I am poison'd"?
9. What starving man is such a humanitarian he tastes nothing until the aged companion in his wanderings is fed?
10. How many Queens of France appear in the plays?
11. Whose "voice was ever soft, Gentle and low, an excellent thing in woman"?
12. Identify the dying Queen who confesses she had planned to poison the King and his daughter, and put her son on the throne.
13. What husband and wife believe each other dead for fourteen years?
14. Who loves a young lady because she pities the dangers he has endured?
15. Name the Goth who says, "She is a woman, therefore may be woo'd; She is a woman, therefore may be won."
16. Who is the woman?
17. Which character is put in a position where he has to go out and find himself a father?
18. Who is the son of the evil blue-eyed dead witch, Sycorax?

19. Which is the shortest of the major tragedies?
20. Name the follower of Falstaff who speaks almost exclusively in verse.

35. "SUNDRY CONTEMPLATIONS"

1. Which King awakens from a coma and is distressed to find his crown is missing?
2. Who claims he is speaking "brotherly" of his brother when he says, "there is not one so young and so villainous this day living"?
3. Identify the following: "Boblibindo chicurmurco."
4. Who "examples" thieves "with thievery" by giving a dissertation on the thefts in nature?
5. Name the newly elected Emperor whose first official act is to set all war prisoners free without ransom.
6. What custom is "More honour'd in the breach than in the observance"?
7. Who, under constraint, agrees to change religions?
8. What young girl willingly changes religions?
9. Which character has already been converted to a new religion when he first appears?
10. How many of the hundred or more Italians in the plays speak English with an Italian accent?
11. At whose trial is an oracle read from the Oracle of Delphos?
12. What miserable and betrayed man laughs because he has no more tears to shed?
13. What girl is forbidden by her father to tell her name but does it inadvertently?
14. In what battle does Falstaff take a dubious part?
15. What three Queens of England appear as widows?

16. Name the girl who goes into a rage whenever her rival calls her "little" and "low."
17. What man, without batting an eye, asks the father of the girl he considers marrying what her dowry will be?
18. Who says the man who stole his throne is "bloody, Luxurious, avaricious, false, deceitful, Sudden, malicious"?
19. Who remarks on the battlefield that slaying is "in fashion"?
20. Having been forbidden to carry weapons, the followers of what two quarrelers fight each other with pebble stones?

36. "SUNDRY CONTEMPLATIONS"

1. In which play is there a Dance of Twelve Satyrs?
2. Who wails, "Reputation, reputation, reputation! O, I have lost my reputation!"?
3. What elderly man boasts of having played the role of Julius Caesar when he was a university student?
4. Who cannot get a song called "Willow" out of her mind?
5. How many Scottish characters speak English with a Scottish accent?
6. Who orders his servant to bring a rope so he can whip his wife and the characters he thinks she has been consorting with?
7. What lady is "The noble sister of Publicola, The moon of Rome; chaste as the icicle"?
8. When one death order is substituted for another by a supposedly insane candidate for murder, what two men die in his place?
9. Who deciphers a message which Jupiter leaves with a man in prison?
10. What Queen loses her country but begs her conqueror to give it back to her for her son?
11. Identify the son.

12. Name the desperate rebel, hiding out in Kent, who deplores the fact that he has a sword and yet is starving to death.
13. What mother, to pacify her son, tells him she can buy twenty husbands in any market?
14. Name the man "Who woo'd in haste, and means to wed at leisure."
15. What warrior, before he dies, loses twenty-four of his twenty-five sons?
16. Who has an exceedingly efficient little helper, whom others can hear but no one can see except himself?
17. In what bit of writing do the following appear: "Helen's cheek," "Cleopatra's majesty," and "Lucretia's modesty"?
18. Who are Simon Catling, Hugh Rebeck and James Soundpost?
19. Who says, "O world! world! world!"?
20. What relation is the Duke of Buckingham to both the Earl of Surrey and Lord Abergavenny?

37. "SUNDRY CONTEMPLATIONS"

1. Who has a spaniel named Troilus?
2. In which play do eleven ghosts of murder victims appear in one scene?
3. Identify the adventurous character who is promised "flapjacks" to eat by a stranger if he will go home with him.
4. What do "Trifles light as air" seem to the jealous?
5. In which play is there a double wedding?
6. Sackerson is the name of an animal that scares the women past belief. What kind of an animal is it?
7. What faithful servant says in the third act of a play that he is going to bed at noon and is never heard of again?
8. Who "has a lean and hungry look"?

9. Identify the only man and woman to be divorced?

10. Who avenges his father's death by killing the young son of his father's slayer?

11. This man, whose father died in exile because of a quarrel with a Duke who became King, joins in a rebellion against the King. Who is he?

12. Who feels like drinking hot blood?

13. Under what circumstances are the following words spoken: "If sight and shape be true, Why then, my love adieu!"?

14. What character is told by her husband that a woman of her "undaunted mettle" should produce only male children?

15. This Prince is given a substantial income by his uncle for promising never to attack Denmark again. Name him.

16. Who has a grandson called Marcius?

17. What "wears out more apparel than the man"?

18. Which mother dies of grief because of her son's exile?

19. Who stops a Queen from stabbing herself, hoping to carry out orders to take her alive?

20. Does Orlando, Macbeth or Hamlet say: "This I must do, or know not what to do: Yet this I will not do, do how I can"?

38. "SUNDRY CONTEMPLATIONS"

1. What is it a philosopher cannot endure patiently?

2. Who, shortly before he dies, says he has a joyful heart because he never, in all his life, found a man false to him?

3. What two erudite men are reported to have been at a "great feast of languages, and stolen the scraps"?

4. Who says to whom, "What's mine is yours, and what is yours is mine"?

5. What murdered man is left in a ditch with twenty "trenched gashes on his head"?

6. Who uses the word "Anthropophaginian"?

7. What two Princesses die because of their love for one man?

8. Who, to atone for his guilt in the reported death of his bride-to-be, is ordered to sing an epitaph at her tomb and marry her cousin?

9. What dying woman tries to protect her guilty husband by declaring she has committed suicide?

10. The ghost of what murdered woman returns briefly to haunt her husband?

11. What Princess is temporarily reduced to earning her living as a teacher of singing, sewing, weaving and dancing?

12. Who practically doubles his daughter's dowry after she learns to act like a lady?

13. Name the two lovers who are discovered in a cave, playing chess.

14. Identify the thieves who are on the verge of becoming honest men after a cynical character encourages them to keep on stealing.

15. What child joins in the avowal of vengeance on the betrayers of his aunt?

16. Whose eye, cheek, lip and foot, all speak?

17. Name the steward who attributes the handwriting in a letter to his mistress, because he recognizes her C's, U's, T's and P's.

18. Who dies chanting "snatches of old tunes"?

19. What male-attired girl tells her fickle lover that for women "to change their shapes" is no worse than for men to change their minds?

20. Which of the English historical plays has a prologue prefacing each act?

39. "SUNDRY CONTEMPLATIONS"

1. Who has "three and thirty wounds" which his heir vows will be avenged?
2. Who is the heir?
3. What fellow is "wise enough to play the fool; And to do that well craves a kind of wit"?
4. Name the dying deserter who calls himself "A master-leaver and a fugitive."
5. Which play has an epilogue spoken by its heroine?
6. Who is "The glass of fashion and the mould of form, The observed of all observers"?
7. What young rebel is killed at the battle of Shrewsbury?
8. What is the only reference made in the plays to Queen Elizabeth as the ruler of England in Shakespeare's time?
9. In which play can the day of the week be determined for each scene?
10. Who "loved not wisely but too well"?
11. Does Falstaff, Macbeth or Thersites say, "Blow, wind! come, wrack! At least we'll die with harness on our back"?
12. What matter is to be settled by "three umpires"?
13. Who sadly regrets that he must give his "large kingdom for a little grave, A little little grave, an obscure grave"?
14. In whose honor do two men promise to erect statues of pure gold?
15. What King is the father of fifty sons?
16. Who has done "a thousand dreadful things," and grieves that he "cannot do ten thousand more"?
17. What army commander orders his soldiers to kill an unarmed enemy and takes credit for it himself?

18. Identify the unarmed enemy.
19. What King tells a man of eighty-three he is sorry he will only be shortening his life a week when he hangs him?
20. Who says, "O, horrible! O, horrible! most horrible!"?

40. "SUNDRY CONTEMPLATIONS"

1. Name the woman who locks herself in a monument to escape the wrath of the lover she has betrayed, and sends him word that she is dead.
2. Identify the famous Roman orator, statesman and senator who is liquidated in a purge.
3. What dying man gives his purse to his slayer with the request to bury him?
4. What King hands a man a group of incriminating papers, tells him to read them, and adds "then to breakfast with What appetite you have"?
5. What gives shapes to things unknown, "A local habitation and a name" to "airy nothing"?
6. What bewildered woman bewails, "I see two husbands, or mine eyes deceive me"?
7. The crest of what family is "The rampant bear chain'd to the ragged staff"?
8. This jealous man pays a rogue to help him make a date with his own wife. Who is he?
9. Watching from a vantage point on a hill, what servant mistakes victory for defeat and changes the outcome of a war?
10. Just what are the "Sweets to the sweet"?
11. Who in speaking of his wife says, "She is my goods, my chattels, my field, my barn, My horse, my ox, my ass, my any thing"?

12. What King goes incognito to a shepherd's sheep-shearing party to spy on his son?
13. Whose dead body is tied to a horse's tail and dragged over the field?
14. What barbarian is to be set "breast-deep in earth" and starved?
15. What man is reported to play with flowers when he is dying?
16. Which "king's a beggar, now the play is done"?
17. Whose "chastity's the jewel" of her house, "Bequeathed down from many ancestors"?
18. What woman is worth a city full of consuls, senators, patricians, and a sea and land full of tribunes?
19. "What is he that builds stronger than either the mason, the shipwright, or the carpenter?" "The houses that he makes last till doomsday."
20. Who says, "Never, never, never, never, never!" and what is meant by it?

(*Measure for Measure*)

PART II

"*Our Special Drift*"

41. "OUR JUST AND LINEAL ENTRANCE"
(*King John*)

Identify twenty heroines and their plays by the following entrance lines.

1. Good Lord Boyet, my beauty, though but mean,
   Needs not the painted flourish of your praise.
2. By my troth, Nerissa, my little body is aweary of this great world.
3. Dear Celia, I show more mirth than I am mistress of.
4. Do you doubt that?
5. How now! who calls?
6. I do affect a sorrow, indeed, but I have it too.
7. If by your art, my dearest father, you have
   Put the wild waters in this roar, allay them.
8. If it be love indeed, tell me how much.
9. In peace and honour live Lord Titus long.
10. I pray you, daughter, sing, or express yourself in a more comfortable sort.
11. I pray you, is Signior Mountanto returned from the wars or no?
12.   My noble father,
    I do perceive here a divided duty.
13. Nay, we must longer kneel: I am a suitor.
14. Neither my husband nor the slave return'd.
15.   O
    Dissembling courtesy! How fine this tyrant
    Can tickle where she wounds!
16. Sir Valentine and servant, to you two thousand.
17. So is Lysander.

18. Take the fool away.
19. I pray you, sir, is it your will
    To make a stale of me amongst these mates?
20. Who were those went by?

42. "ADMIT HIM ENTRANCE" (*Henry VIII*)

Identify twenty heroes by the following entrance lines.
  1. Hail, Rome, victorious in thy mourning weeds!
  2. Attend the lords of France and Burgundy, Gloucester.
  3. Your faithful subject I, a gentleman
     Born in Northamptonshire.
  4. Where is my gracious Lord of Canterbury?
  5. My liege, I did deny no prisoners.
  6.   Be collected:
     No more amazement: tell your piteous heart
     There's no harm done.
  7. Thanks. What's the matter, you dissentious rogues.
  8. As I remember it, Adam, it was upon this fashion.
  9. Cease to persuade, my loving Proteus.
 10. Imprison'd is he, say you?
 11. 'Tis better as it is.
 12. So foul and fair a day I have not seen.
 13. Escalus.
 14. You have her father's love, Demetrius.
 15. I have, Antiochus, and, with a soul
     Embolden'd with the glory of her praise.
 16. Verona, for a while I take my leave.
 17. Call here my varlet; I'll unarm again.
 18. There's beggary in the love that can be reckon'd.
 19. Is the day so young?
 20. A little more than kin, and less than kind.

43. "BY ANY OTHER NAME" (*Romeo and Juliet*)

Please match the characters on the left with their assumed
names on the right, and give the names of the plays in which
they appear.

1. Arviragus	( ) _____	*a.* Aliena
2. Belarius	( ) _____	*b.* Cadwal
3. Celia	( ) _____	*c.* Caius
4. Earl of Kent	( ) _____	*d.* Cambio
5. Edgar	( ) _____	*e.* Cesario
6. Florizel	( ) _____	*f.* Doctor Balthasar
7. Guiderius	( ) _____	*g.* Doricles
8. Henry V	( ) _____	*h.* Fidele
9. Hortensio	( ) _____	*i.* Friar Lodowick
10. Imogen	( ) _____	*j.* Ganymede
11. Jack Cade	( ) _____	*k.* Harry le Roy
12. Julia	( ) _____	*l.* Sir John Mortimer
13. Lucentio	( ) _____	*m.* Licio
14. Ford	( ) _____	*n.* Lucentio
15. Portia	( ) _____	*o.* Master Brook
16. Rosalind	( ) _____	*p.* Morgan
17. Sebastian	( ) _____	*q.* Polydore
18. Tranio	( ) _____	*r.* Roderigo
19. Vincentio	( ) _____	*s.* Sebastian
20. Viola	( ) _____	*t.* Poor Tom

44. "BRIDES AND BRIDEGROOMS ALL" Number 1
(*As You Like It*)

Match the couples who are married during the action of the
plays or are about to be when the plays end.

1. Lady Anne   (   ) _____   *a.* Bassianus
2. Anne Bullen   (   ) _____   *b.* Benedick
3. Audrey   (   ) _____   *c.* Claudio
4. Beatrice   (   ) _____   *d.* Demetrius
5. Bianca   (   ) _____   *e.* Edward IV
6. Blanch   (   ) _____   *f.* Ferdinand
7. Celia   (   ) _____   *g.* Florizel
8. Cordelia   (   ) _____   *h.* Henry V
9. Lady Grey   (   ) _____   *i.* Henry VIII
10. Helena   (   ) _____   *j.* King of France
11. Isabella   (   ) _____   *k.* Lewis
12. Jessica   (   ) _____   *l.* Lorenzo
13. Julia   (   ) _____   *m.* Lucentio
14. Juliet   (   ) _____   *n.* Lysimachus
15. Katharine   (   ) _____   *o.* Oliver
16. Lavinia   (   ) _____   *p.* Orsino
17. Marina   (   ) _____   *q.* Proteus
18. Miranda   (   ) _____   *r.* Richard III
19. Perdita   (   ) _____   *s.* Touchstone
20. Viola   (   ) _____   *t.* Vincentio

45. "BRIDES AND BRIDEGROOMS ALL" Number 2

1. Anne Page   (   ) _____   *a.* Angelo
2. Helena   (   ) _____   *b.* Antipholus of Syracuse
3. Hermia   (   ) _____   *c.* Antony
4. Hero   (   ) _____   *d.* Bassanio
5. Hippolyta   (   ) _____   *e.* Bertram
6. Katharina   (   ) _____   *f.* Camillo
7. Luciana   (   ) _____   *g.* Claudio
8. Margaret   (   ) _____   *h.* Fenton

9. Mariana	( ) _____	*i.* Gratiano
10. Nerissa	( ) _____	*j.* Henry VI
11. Octavia	( ) _____	*k.* Sir Toby
12. Olivia	( ) _____	*l.* Lysander
13. Paulina	( ) _____	*m.* Orlando
14. Phebe	( ) _____	*n.* Pericles
15. Portia	( ) _____	*o.* Petruchio
16. Rosalind	( ) _____	*p.* Saturninus
17. Silvia	( ) _____	*q.* Sebastian
18. Tamora	( ) _____	*r.* Silvius
19. Thaisa	( ) _____	*s.* Theseus
20. Maria	( ) _____	*t.* Valentine

46. "ALONE I DID IT" (*Coriolanus*)

Here are the beginning lines. Name the soliloquizers.
1. The regent conquers, and the Frenchmen fly.
2. O, were that all! I think not on my father.
3. Peace, you ungracious clamours! peace, rude sounds!
   Fools on both sides!
4. A goodly city is this Antium. City,
   'Tis I that made thy widows.
5. If I be not ashamed of my soldiers, I am a soused gur-
   net.
6. O, what a rogue and peasant slave am I!
7. Gallop apace, you fiery-footed steeds.
8. Most welcome, bondage! for thou art a way,
   I think, to liberty.
9. No care, no stop! so senseless of expense.
10. Thus do I ever make my fool my purse.
11. How use doth breed a habit in a man!

12. There's not a man I meet but doth salute me
    As if I were their well-acquainted friend.
13. This is the air; that is the glorious sun;
    This pearl she gave me, I do feel 't and see 't.
14. When I would pray and think, I think and pray.
15. I came from England as ambassador,
    But I return his sworn and mortal foe.
16. Now climbeth Tamora Olympus' top.
17. The king he is hunting the deer; I am coursing myself.
18. All the infections that the sun sucks up
    From bogs, fens, flats, on Prosper fall.
19. A foot of honour better than I was;
    But many a many foot of land the worse.
20. If it were done when 'tis done, then 'twere well
    It were done quickly.

47. "THE BITTER BREAD OF BANISHMENT"
(*Richard II*)

You are to identify the twenty banished characters referred to.

1. This Duke, who thoroughly enjoys his banishment, establishes his home in the woods and soon has a collection of characters.
2. He is expelled from Athens by the Senate for pleading the case of a friend who has killed a man in a brawl.
3. When this villainous Englishman goes into banishment he takes the Queen's heart with him.
4. This Roman hero is elected Consul but is driven from his country before he has an opportunity to serve.
5. She is banished by her father because she lacks "that glib and oily art, To speak and purpose not."
6. When he is expatriated by the King, this forty-year-old

Duke bemoans the fact that he will have to learn a new language.

7. Exiled from England on pain of death, this Queen returns because she finds more pain in banishment than in the threat of death.

8. This banished member of a tortured Roman family joins the Goths and leads a victorious army against Rome.

9. He is ostracized by the Duke of Milan for attempting to elope with his daughter.

10. This bridegroom is banished by his father-in-law whose parting words to him are: "away! Thou'rt poison to my blood."

11. This former companion of a newly crowned King is forbidden to come within ten miles of him.

12. Having been falsely accused of treason, this bitter banished lord took the King's infant sons into exile with him.

13. This coward is banished by Henry VI, his knighthood repealed, and his garter plucked from his leg.

14. On her way to exile, this woman is forced to walk barefoot in public and wrapped in a white sheet.

15. This titled nobleman, after being banished by the King, returns disguised and becomes his servant.

16. Julius Caesar banished this man and will not recall him although his brother and others plead for him.

17. Banished by Richard II, he returns before the expiration of his time and usurps the King's crown.

18. This new husband is banished when he kills his bride's cousin.

19. This banished man cleverly traps his banishers, punishes them, and then makes friends with them.

20. This girl is banished by her uncle so that his daughter will "show more bright and seem more virtuous When she is gone."

48. "THAT OLD AND ANTIQUE SONG"
(*Twelfth Night*)

Identify twenty "songbirds" by the following first lines.

1. Do nothing but eat, and make good cheer.
2. To shallow rivers, to whose falls.
3. Sigh no more, ladies, sigh no more.
4. Full fathom five thy father lies.
5. The ousel cock, so black of hue.
6. Blow, blow, thou winter wind.
7. Was this fair face the cause, quoth she.
8. Lawn as white as driven snow.
9. Fear no more the heat o' the sun.
10. Fools had ne'er less wit in a year.
11. An old hare hoar.
12. To-morrow is Saint Valentine's day.
13. King Stephen was a worthy peer.
14. Love, love, nothing but love, still more!
15. Orpheus with his lute made trees.
16. The master, the swabber, the boatswain, and I.
17. O Mistress mine, where are you roaming?
18. Farewell, master; farewell, farewell!
19. Knocks go and come; God's vassals drop and die.
20. Take, O, take those lips away.

49. "INSULTED, RAIL'D, AND PUT UPON"
(*King Lear*)

Identify the insulter and the insulted by each of the following quotations?

1. Shut your mouth, dame.
2.   You are more intemperate in your blood
   Than Venus.
3. I think thee now some common customer.
4. O faithless coward! O dishonest wretch!
   Wilt thou be made a man out of my vice?
5. Thou picture of what thou seemest, and idol of idiot
   worshippers.
6. I do desire we may be better strangers.
7. Vanish, or I shall give thee thy deserving.
8. Dissembling harlot, thou art false in all,
   And art confederate with a damned pack.
9. Thou art a most pernicious usurer,
   Froward by nature, enemy to peace;
   Lascivious, wanton.
10.   Thou art like the harpy,
    Which, to betray, dost, with thine angel's face,
    Seize with thine eagle's talons.
11. There's no more faith in thee than in a stewed prune.
12. Could I come near your beauty with my nails,
    I'ld set my ten commandments in your face.
13. You lisp, and nick-name God's creatures, and make your
    wantonness your ignorance.
14.   Peace, you mumbling fool!
    Utter your gravity o'er a gossip's bowl.
15.   You yourself
    Are much condemn'd to have an itching palm.
16.   I hate thee,
    Pronounce thee a gross lout, a mindless slave.
17. Thou little valiant, great in villainy!
    Thou ever strong upon the stronger side!
18. Fie, fie! you counterfeit, you puppet, you!
19. Ah, my sour husband, my hard-hearted lord.

20. Away, thou issue of a mangy dog!
    Choler does kill me that thou art alive.

50. "WITH CUSTOMARY COMPLIMENT"
(*The Winter's Tale*)

Identify the complimenter and the complimented by each of
the following quotations. There may be a flatterer or two.

  1. My purse, my person, my extremest means,
    Lie all unlock'd to your occasions.
  2.   Thou art fair, and at thy birth, dear boy,
    Nature and Fortune join'd to make thee great.
  3.   I have loved you night and day
    For many weary months.
  4. Thy deeds, thy plainness and thy housekeeping,
    Hath won the greatest favour of the commons.
  5. Well said, old mole!
  6. Thou art the best o' the cut-throats.
  7. I see how thine eye would emulate the diamond.
  8.   Though mine enemy thou hast ever been,
    High sparks of honour in thee have I seen.
  9. An angel is like you, Kate, and you are like an angel.
  10. Now, my good sweet honey lord, ride with us to-morrow.
  11. Sir, I love you more than words can wield the matter;
    Dearer than eye-sight, space and liberty.
  12. Thine eyes, sweet lady, have infected mine.
  13.   Thee,
    That art to me as secret and as dear
    As Anna to the Queen of Carthage was.
  14. That which I show, heaven knows, is merely love,
    Duty and zeal to your unmatched mind.

15. Our care and pity is so much upon you
    That we remain your friend.

16.   I love thee; I have spoke it:
    How much the quantity, the weight as much,
    As I do love my father.

17. But love thee better than thou canst devise
    Till thou shalt know the reason of my love.

18. The fairest hand I ever touch'd! O beauty,
    Till now I never knew thee!

19. Thou noble thing! more dances my rapt heart
    Than when I first my wedded mistress saw
    Bestride my threshold.

20. You are my true and honourable wife,
    As dear to me as are the ruddy drops
    That visit my sad heart.

51. "ANSWER ME IN ONE WORD" (*As You Like It*)

1. What word has no woman ever heard courteous Antony
   speak?

2. Touchstone says this word is the only peace-maker.

3. When Coriolanus is preparing to face the accusations of
   the people what word does he promise to remember in
   answering them?

4. What word does Macbeth find impossible to say immediately after Duncan's murder?

5. When Edmund is soliloquizing on his position as the nat-
   ural son of Gloucester, what does he think is a very fine
   word?

6. When Hamlet sends a letter to the King telling him he

is returning from his planned trip to England, which word in the postscript baffles Claudius?

7. Portia complains that this word is forbidden to her but not to her suitors.

8. If the Duchess of York were Bolingbroke's nurse, what is the first word she would teach him to say?

9. Juliet laments that this word "hath slain ten thousand Tybalts."

10. What word does Sir Toby Belch use that Sir Andrew Aguecheek mistakes for Maria's name?

11. What word does the Earl of Douglas say is not "Spoke of in Scotland"?

12. After Countess Rousillon says: "This young gentlewoman had a father," which word does she repeat and stress with sorrow?

13. What does Sir William Lucy say "is a mere French word; We English warriors wot not what it means"?

14. What does Bardolph consider "a soldier-like word" and of "good command"?

15. Whenever anyone uses this word in connection with Hermione, Leontes objects.

16. The "urging" of what word "hath bred a kind of remorse" in one of the murderers of the Duke of Clarence?

17. What does Richard III say "is but a word that cowards use, Devised at first to keep the strong in awe"?

18. When Morton is reporting to Northumberland on Hotspur's defeat, he tells him this word "did divide The action of their bodies from their souls."

19. What does Falstaff say is only a word? "A trim reckoning! Who hath it? he that died o' Wednesday"?

20. When Bolingbroke leaves for France, what word does Aumerle refrain from saying to him because it would not add years to his banishment?

52. "O MY PROPHETIC SOUL!" (*Hamlet*)

Name the prophets along with the plays in which they prophesy.

1. Methinks I see thee, now thou art below,
   As one dead in the bottom of a tomb.
2. In her days every man shall eat in safety.
3. But I do prophesy the election lights
   On Fortinbras.
4. Thou shalt get kings, though thou be none.
5.   How many ages hence
   Shall this our lofty scene be acted over.
6. His rash fierce blaze of riot cannot last.
7. She has deceived her father, and may thee.
8. Joan la Pucelle shall be France's saint.
9. This pretty lad will prove our country's bliss.
10. I will lay odds that, ere this year expire,
    We bear our civil swords and native fire
    As far as France.
11. A solemn combination shall be made
    Of our dear souls.
12. No grave upon the earth shall clip in it
    A pair so famous.
13. The fall of every Phrygian stone will cost
    A drop of Grecian blood.
14.   Good king, look to 't in time;
    She'll hamper thee, and dandle thee like a baby.
15. If once he come to be a cardinal,
    He'll make his cap co-equal with the crown.
16.   He shall think that thou, which know'st the way
    To plant unrightful kings, wilt know again.

17. This prophecy Merlin shall make; for I live before his time.

18.   Before Ascension-day at noon
    My crown I should give off.

19. O, Warwick, Warwick! I foresee with grief
    The utter loss of all the realm of France.

20. I have a journey, sir, shortly to go;
    My master calls me, I must not say no.

53. "A QUESTION TO BE ASKED" (*Henry IV, Part I*)

Name the character who asks each of the following questions, some of which are rhetorical. All are direct quotations.

1. What, have I choked you with an argosy?

2. Hear you this Triton of the minnows? mark you
   His absolute 'shall'?

3. What! shall they seek the lion in his den,
   And fright him there?

4. Am not I consanguineous? am I not of her blood?

5. Why should I play the Roman fool, and die
   On mine own sword?

6. Is love a generation of vipers?

7. Well, then, go you into hell?

8. Have I lived to stand at the taunt of one that makes
   fritters of English?

9. How art thou out of breath, when thou hast breath
   To say to me that thou art out of breath?

10. Wouldst thou have thy head broken?

11. Knock, knock! Who's there?

12. Think you a little din can daunt mine ears?
    Have I not in my time heard lions roar?

13. What wouldst thou think of me, if I should weep?

14. Where are your mess of sons to back you now?
    The wanton Edward, and the lusty George?
15. Have I a tongue to doom my brother's death,
    And shall that tongue give pardon to a slave?
16. Hast thou given all to thy two daughters?
17. Was the crown offered him thrice?
18.   Is man so hateful to thee,
    That art thyself a man?
19. Madam, how like you this play?
20. Do you confess the bond?

54. "IN SELF-ADMISSION" (*Troilus and Cressida*)

Identify the characters who evaluate themselves in the following quotations.

1. I am nothing if not critical.
2. I am the very pink of courtesy.
3.   I am by birth a shepherd's daughter,
   My wit untrain'd in any kind of art.
4.   I have
   Immortal longings in me.
5.   Though I am not splenitive and rash,
   Yet I have in me something dangerous.
6.   The full sum of me
   Is sum of something, which, to term in gross,
   Is an unlesson'd girl, unschool'd, unpractised.
7.   All the courses of my life do show
   I am not in the roll of common men.
8. My nativity was under Ursa major; so that it follows
   I am rough and lecherous.
9.   I am weaker than a woman's tear,
   Tamer than sleep, fonder than ignorance.

10. I would that I were laid low in my grave:
    I am not worth this coil that's made for me.
11. I am more an antique Roman than a Dane.
12. Though I am not naturally honest, I am so sometimes by chance.
13. I am a very foolish fond old man.
14. I to myself am dearer than a friend.
15. But I am constant as the northern star,
    Of whose true-fix'd and resting quality
    There is no fellow in the firmament.
16. I am a bastard begot, bastard instructed, bastard in mind, bastard in valour, in everything illegitimate.
17. I am misanthropos, and hate mankind.
18. I am not only witty in myself, but the cause that wit is in other men.
19. Though I cannot be said to be a flattering honest man, it must not be denied but I am a plain-dealing villain.
20. I am rough and woo not like a babe.

55. "SUCH STUFF AS DREAMS" (*The Tempest*)

You are to dream up the names of these dreamers.
1. He dreams the clouds "open, and show riches ready to drop" on him, and when he wakes he cries to dream again.
2. This innocent man dreams he feasts with Caesar, and is murdered the next day.
3. He sees in a vision the Roman eagle flying north by west into the sunbeams and this means to him a Roman victory.
4. In his dream his bride finds him dead and when she revives him with kisses, he is an emperor.

5. Imprisoned in the Tower of London, he dreams he is drowning and sees "a thousand fearful wrecks."
6. This Duchess dreams she is sitting in the coronation chair while the King and Queen put the crown on her head.
7. He thinks his daughter's elopement is not unlike his dream.
8. This girl dreams a serpent eats her heart away while her sweetheart watches and smiles.
9. Every night he dreams that he and his foe have each other by the throat, and always awakens "half dead with nothing."
10. This dethroned Queen dreams of six dancers, dressed in white robes, passing garlands of bays to one another.
11. This man dreams of money-bags and knows there is "ill a-brewing."
12. The night before a battle, this man dreams he is cheered on to victory by the ghosts of those his enemy has murdered.
13. This somnambulist sleeps with her eyes open and sees spots.
14. Diana appears to this man in a vision with instructions that lead to a reunion with his wife.
15. This man, who grew up an orphan, sees his mother and father for the first time in a dream.
16. This Athenian dreams of a silver basin and ewer, which he interprets to mean he is to receive a gift—but is wrong.
17. She dreams her husband's statue gushes blood like a fountain.
18. This wife of a great warrior dreams of "bloody turbulence" and the night has "nothing been but shapes and forms of slaughter."
19. In this Cardinal's dream the Duke of Gloucester is dumb and cannot speak a word.

20. He has "a dream, past the wit of man to say what dream it was," and is going to have a ballad written about it.

56. "KNOW YOU THIS RING?"
(*All's Well That Ends Well*)

Please answer these twenty questions concerning rings.

1. Who trades an exceptional turquoise ring for a monkey?
2. In what contest does "he that runs fastest" get the ring?
3. What fickle young man asks his disguised sweetheart to deliver the ring, which she had given him, as a gift to another girl?
4. Which couple is married with a double-ring ceremony?
5. What murdered man is recognized at the bottom of a pit by his ring which illuminates the dark?
6. This young man sends a ring by Mistress Quickly to a girl, whose parents disapprove of him.
7. Who accepts an engagement ring from the admitted murderer of her husband and her father-in-law?
8. Whose mutilated body is identified by his wife when she sees his rings and handkerchief?
9. What two disguised women subtly manage to get rings from their husbands who had sworn never to part with them?
10. In order to find out who gave him a ring, this man is instructed to show it to the Queen of France.
11. What King gives his son-in-law, whom he never sees again, a ring as a parting gift?
12. What disguised girl realizes that a Countess has fallen in love with her when a servant brings her the Countess's ring?

13. This King becomes "wrapp'd in dismal thinkings" when he discovers the ring he had given a bride, in the bridegroom's possession.

14. Which Archbishop is protected at his trial by a ring the King gave him?

15. Who comes to the tomb of his wife "to take thence from her dead finger" a ring that he "must use In dear employment"?

16. What male-clad girl convinces her beloved that she is herself and not a boy when she shows him the rings they had exchanged?

17. Who risks a cudgeling by Falstaff for saying his seal-ring is copper?

18. Where is the line, "In the spring time, the only pretty ring time"?

19. What woman is extremely perturbed because the man who "took perforce" her rare ring has not given her the chain he promised her?

20. Who bets the diamond ring his wife gave him that she is faithful?

57. "THUS MUCH MONEYS"
(*The Merchant of Venice*)

Identify the various amounts and denominations of money.

1. Mistress Ford is reported to rule her husband's purse and what money?

2. Parolles is lying when he says Bertram will sell "the fee-simple of his salvation" for this coin.

3. What indefinite amount does Pandar of Mytilene think would be enough to retire on?

4. Orlando is left this sum in his father's will.

5. What money does Desdemona say she would rather lose than the handkerchief Othello gave her?

6. Christopher Sly is unwilling to pay even this trifle for the glasses he broke belonging to the Hostess.

7. When the Duke of Gloucester is charged with keeping soldiers' pay, he challenges his accusers to prove he took as much as either of these coins.

8. The King of Norway is required to pay this amount to Scotland as part of peace terms.

9. How much money does Julius Caesar leave in his will to each citizen of Rome?

10. Antonio's bond to Shylock is for what amount?

11. Merchants who come to Syracuse from Ephesus lose their lives if they lack this kind of money to redeem themselves.

12. King John gives Blanch this generous sum as part of her dowry when she marries the Dauphin.

13. How much of the King's money does Bolingbroke accuse Mowbray of squandering?

14. Joan of Arc's father gave this to the priest the day he married her mother.

15. Henry IV insists he will not give this trifle to ransom Mortimer.

16. Anne Bullen is given this annual support along with a new title.

17. Nym wins this amount betting with Pistol.

18. Sir Andrew Aguecheek sends this to Feste for his "leman."

19. Overly optimistic Timon of Athens sends servants to three of his associates to borrow this amount.

20. When Flaminius is offered a bribe by Lucullus for pretending he has not seen him, he throws it back at him. How much is it?

58. "A MINT OF PHRASES" Number 1
(*Love's Labour's Lost*)

Fill in the blank spaces with familiar phrases.

1. Let us make an honourable retreat; though not with
. . . . yet with scrip and scrippage.
2. Whilst, like a puff'd and reckless libertine,
Himself . . . . of dalliance treads.
3. True it is that . . . .
And have with holy bell been knoll'd to church.
4. To . . . .
And live, as we do, in this wilderness?
5. What though . . . . thou hast
mettle enough in thee to kill care.
6. As plain as the plain bald pate of . . . . himself.
7. Revisit'st thus the . . . .
Making night hideous.
8. . . . . in lovers meeting.
9. Be thou as chaste as ice, ... thou
shalt not escape calumny.
10. To . . . . oft cures the worse.
11. Nay, if thy wits run the . . . .-. . . . .
I have done.
12. I cannot tell . . . . his name is my
husband had him of.
13. And if you . . . . and do this feat,
Achieve the elder, set the younger free.
14. Thee I'll chase hence, thou . . . . ' .
. . . . .
Out, tawny coats! out, scarlet hypocrite!

15. If we do meet again, why . . . .
    If not, why then this parting was well made.
16. . . . . shall not drive me back,
    When gold and silver becks me to come on.
17. I'll answer him by law: . ' . .   . .
    . . . . boy: let him come, and kindly.
18. And . . .   . have lighted fools
    The way to dusty death.
19. Though thou canst . . . . thou art
    made like a goose.
20. Then, if he lose, he makes .   . . . .˜. . . .   . . .
    Fading in music.

59. "A MINT OF PHRASES" Number 2

1. My friends were . . . . so's my love.
2. Turn him to any cause of policy,
   . . .   . of it he will unloose.
3.   It is a tale
   Told by an idiot, full of . . . .
   Signifying nothing.
4. And . . . . that takes survey of all the world,
   . . . .
5. Life is as tedious as .   . . . . .˜. . . .   .
   Vexing the dull ear of a drowsy man.
6. There is . . . . that we cannot get in.
7. The smallest . . . . being trodden on.
8.   Yet do I fear thy nature;
   It is too full o' . . .   .˜
   . . . .
   To catch the nearest way.

9. This lanthorn doth the horned moon present;
   Myself . . . . ' . . . . do seem to be.
10. What, must I . . . . to my shames?
11. Ay, marry, now my soul hath . . . .
    It would not out at windows nor at doors.
12. That which in mean men we intitle patience
    Is . . . . in noble breasts.
13. If ye should lead her into . . . . . ' . . . . **as**
    they say, it were a very gross kind of behaviour.
14. We will have rings, and things, and fine array;
    And . . . . we will be married o' Sunday.
15. The devil can . . . . for his purpose.
16. Well, every one can . . . . but he that
    has it.
17.   The joiner squirrel or old grub,
    . . . . ' . . . . the fairies' coachmakers.
18. This is a way to . . . .-
    . . . .
    And thus I'll curb her mad and headstrong humour.
19. I have been . . . . since I saw **you**
    last, that, I fear me, will never out of my bones.
20. Now cracks a noble heart. . . . .
    . . . . . .
    And flights of angels sing thee to thy rest!

60. "A MINT OF PHRASES" Number 3

1. Why doth the great Duke Humphrey . . . .
   . . . . .
   As frowning at the favours of the world?
2. . . . . I have not heard the clock.
3. Whither, my lord? from . . . .
   Lord Talbot.

4.   Now, by . . .-. . . . .
Nature hath framed strange fellows in her time.

5. His speech was . . . . nothing impaired, but all disordered.

6. To be a well-favoured man is . . . .
. . . . but to write and read comes by nature.

7. Not in my house, Lucentio; for, you know,
. . . . and I have many servants.

8. . . . . I like the cap;
And it I will have, or I will have none.

9. 'Tis not enough . . . .
But to support him after.

10.   Then . . . .-. .
Grace and good disposition attend your ladyship!

11. I would have such a fellow whipped for o'erdoing Ter-
magant; it . . .-. . . . . pray you, avoid it.

12. I could . . . . with his lady's fan.

13.   If ladies be but . . . .
They have the gift to know it.

14. There have been many great men that have . . . .
. . . . who ne'er loved them.

15. Give me my Romeo; and, when he shall die,
Take him and . . . . in little stars.

16. If you desire the spleen, and will . . . .
. . . . follow me.

17. Yet, spaniel-like, the more . . . .
The more it grows.

18. If I do not leave you all as . . . .-. . . .
I pray God I may never eat grass more.

19. I am . . . . my lord, but not so patient.

20. Small cheer and . . . . makes a merry
feast.

61. "BEING ABSENT HENCE"
(*The Merchant of Venice*)

You are to identify these off-stage characters.

1. This daughter of Priam captures the heart of Achilles.
2. Henry VII marries this daughter of Edward IV.
3. She is all set to marry a French Count when his reportedly dead wife returns.
4. Her "rags, and the tallow in them, will burn a Poland winter."
5. This Emperor declares war on Britain because of an unpaid tribute, loses the war, but receives the tribute nevertheless.
6. This Norman is "the brooch indeed And gem of all the nation," and he highly recommends the fencing of Laertes.
7. When a marriage is being considered for this English Princess, the question of her legitimacy causes her father to develop scruples.
8. King John is excommunicated from the church when he refuses to install this man as Archbishop of Canterbury.
9. This Queen has just gone by with a companion when the curtain goes up.
10. This gentlewoman reports that she heard Celia and Rosalind speak admiringly of Orlando and is sure the three have run away together.
11. He gives instructions and furnishes the robes to aid Portia in becoming a lawyer.
12. This woman, whom Lucio is forced to marry, is the mother of an illegitimate child, "a year and a quarter old, come Philip and Jacob."

13. She never shows her face but is so hated that the man who is disguised in her clothes receives a sound beating.
14. This fellow, who "was perfumed like a milliner," would have been a soldier except for the "vile guns."
15. This daughter of the Governor of Tarsus is at such disadvantage when compared to her parents' ward, her mother plots to have the ward murdered.
16. She is the mistress of Edward IV.
17. This deserted wife dies in the first act.
18. This lady, her admirer says, is "too fair, too wise, wisely too fair."
19. Because of the marriage of this Princess to the King of Tunis, her father and his retinue are trapped on a strange island.
20. This King of England gives asylum to a Scottish Prince.

PART III

Play by Play Department

"FOUR CORNERS
OF THE EARTH"

(The Merchant of Venice)

62. TROILUS AND CRESSIDA

1. How long has the Trojan war been going on?
2. According to Pandarus, whose helmet is "more hacked than Hector's"?
3. Which Greek does Aeneas call "the high and mighty"?
4. Which of the Trojan Princes is a priest?
5. Name the Greek who sounds off with a slanderous tongue intermittently throughout the play.
6. Who thinks Helen is not worth what she costs and wants to call the whole thing off?
7. The holding captive by the Greeks of what Trojan woman gave Paris his excuse for abducting Helen?
8. The only woman worthy of being called a prophetess is in this play. Name her.
9. Who arranges the clandestine meeting of Troilus and Cressida?
10. What does Calchas ask of Agamemnon in return for his services to the Greek army?
11. Who is sent to tell Cressida she must leave Troy and Troilus?

12. What is Pandarus talking about when he says: "What a pair of spectacles is here!"?

13. Who conducts Cressida to the Grecian camp and rouses Troilus' jealousy?

14. How do the Greek leaders welcome Cressida to their camp?

15. Which of Priam's sons is the youngest?

16. Why does Hector refuse to fight Ajax?

17. Who leads Troilus to Calchas' tent?

18. What token does Cressida give her new lover, which Troilus had given her?

19. Whose horse is named Galathe?

20. What spurs Achilles to action after his long period of inactivity?

63. *PERICLES*

1. In what country is Antioch, where Antiochus rules?

2. How does Antiochus eliminate the wooers of his daughter?

3. What does Pericles bring to Tarsus that makes him more than welcome?

4. Still fleeing from his pursuer and having been shipwrecked in a storm, where does our hero turn up, soaking wet?

5. How does Pericles win Thaisa for his bride?

6. What news does a messenger bring that makes it possible for Pericles to return to Tyre?

7. Believing Thaisa dead, what do the sailors insist must be done before the raging storm will be appeased?

8. Where does Thaisa turn up, encased but very much alive?

9. Why does Pericles name his new-born daughter Marina?

10. With whom does Pericles leave Marina on his way to Tyre?

11. How old is Marina when we meet her again?

12. How is Marina saved from being murdered?
13. To whom do the kidnappers sell poor Marina?
14. What noble influence does Marina have on the men who visit her in the brothel?
15. Who helps Marina out of her terrible predicament by giving her money?
16. What makes Pericles so reluctant to believe his daughter is standing before him?
17. What does Pericles call the music he alone hears?
18. How does Thaisa greet her long lost husband?
19. What does Pericles promise to do to improve his appearance that he has neglected for fourteen years?
20. Where will Thaisa and Pericles spend the rest of their lives?

64. TIMON OF ATHENS

1. Of what ilk are the majority of Timon's associates?
2. Whom does Timon free from prison by paying his debts?
3. Who says grace at Timon's elaborate banquet?
4. What group appears to entertain the guests with singing and dancing?
5. Who openly warns Timon against his extravagances?
6. Which member of Timon's household is the first to realize he is bankrupt?
7. Name the soldier who is a true friend of Timon's.
8. Where does Timon expect to get the money to pay his debts?
9. When Timon attempts to borrow the money, who pretends to be angry because Timon appealed to him last?
10. When Timon invites his friends to a second banquet, what do they agree was his reason for trying to borrow money?
11. What food is served at the second banquet?

12. Who divides what wealth he has with his fellow servants?
13. Where does Timon go to live?
14. Why does Timon give Alcibiades some of the gold he has found?
15. Who swears he loves Timon better in his impecunious state?
16. After the news has been spread that Timon has gold, which two characters arrive eager to get some of it before it is all gone?
17. Who is the only person Timon considers honest and is civil to?
18. Why do the Senators want Timon to return to Athens?
19. Who are the only people, Alcibiades agrees, to be punished if he is allowed to enter the gates of Athens peaceably?
20. How does an illiterate soldier copy the inscription on Timon's tomb?

65. CYMBELINE

1. Who had been selected by the King and Queen to be Imogen's husband?
2. Whom has Imogen married, upsetting Cymbeline and his whole court?
3. Where has the orphaned Posthumus grown up?
4. Name the two members of the royal family who disappeared twenty years ago.
5. Where does Posthumus go after Cymbeline drives him out?
6. When the Queen asks the doctor for his most poisonous drugs, what does he give her?
7. What song does Cloten have the musicians render to help him win the affections of Imogen?
8. How does Iachimo convince Posthumus of Imogen's infidelity?

9. Who is Emperor of Rome at this time?
10. Who, according to Cymbeline, was the first King of Britain?
11. Who knighted Cymbeline?
12. Having been convinced by Iachimo that Imogen is false, whom does deceived Posthumus order to murder her?
13. Who is the real heir to the throne of Britain?
14. Who is "all the comfort The gods will diet" Imogen with?
15. When Imogen is trying to get to Milford-Haven, in whose cave does she stop to rest?
16. Why does Imogen appear dead to her brothers and Belarius?
17. Why does Imogen mistake Cloten's headless body for her husband's?
18. What does Posthumus receive which convinces him that Imogen is dead?
19. When Cymbeline is captured in battle by the Romans, who are his rescuers?
20. What birthmark does Guiderius have on his neck that identifies him?

"AS OUR ROMAN
ACTORS DO"

(*Julius Caesar*)

66. CORIOLANUS

1. What does one of the rebels say the citizens of Rome would get at their own price if they killed Caius Marcius?
2. What friend of Caius Marcius do the citizens agree is an honest and worthy man?
3. Who is "a lion" that Marcius is proud to hunt?
4. Who is Marcius' commander?
5. What city is the headquarters of the Volsces?
6. Who appears to be the only person concerned with whether or not Marcius might be killed?
7. What effect does Valeria say the yarn that Penelope spun had on Ithaca?
8. Why is Marcius given the title of Coriolanus?
9. What is the first thing Coriolanus says after he has been given the title?
10. When Coriolanus demands that a poor prisoner who had been kind to him be released, why aren't his orders obeyed?
11. Who thanks the gods that Coriolanus is coming home wounded and loves to talk about his scars?

12. How does Menenius feel about Coriolanus' wounds?
13. Name the famous enemy of Rome that Coriolanus, at the age of sixteen, encountered on the battlefield and "struck him on his knee."
14. On being elected Consul what is Coriolanus required to do that is especially distasteful to him?
15. Name the Volscian spy and the Roman traitor who meet on the highway between Rome and Antium and exchange information?
16. With whom does Coriolanus join forces against Rome after he has been betrayed?
17. Name the two rabble rousers who poison the minds of the Roman citizens.
18. While the rebels are patting each other on the back for bringing peace to Rome, what startling news is brought them?
19. Who persuades Coriolanus to give up the siege?
20. What does Aufidius call Coriolanus that enrages him?

67. JULIUS CAESAR

1. What holiday is being celebrated the day the play begins?
2. Who tells Caesar to "Beware the Ides of March"?
3. Besides being an epileptic, what minor infirmity does Caesar have?
4. Who offers the crown to Caesar?
5. Who appears most reluctant to join the conspirators, but has already reasoned to himself that Caesar must die?
6. What important man is left out of the conspiracy because it is decided that he will not join in anything he does not start himself?
7. Whom besides Caesar does Cassius suggest for extermination?

8. Who talks Caesar into going to the Senate after Calpurnia has convinced him he should stay at home?
9. Which of the conspirators, according to plan, draws Mark Antony away from the scene of the murder beforehand?
10. Who is the first to stab Caesar?
11. Where does Mark Antony go immediately after the assassination?
12. Who futilely objects to Antony's being allowed to speak at the funeral?
13. Whom had Caesar invited to Rome and is seven leagues away?
14. On what occasion does Brutus say: "I had rather be a dog, and bay the moon, Than such a Roman"?
15. Which character has the most lines in this play?
16. Who is the only person to see Caesar's ghost?
17. What physical weakness does Cassius have?
18. Whom does Cassius order to stab him?
19. Who holds Brutus' sword while he runs on it?
20. Who says Brutus "was the noblest Roman of them all"?

68. *ANTONY AND CLEOPATRA*

1. What, according to Philo, has Antony been transformed into?
2. How does the Soothsayer tell the fortunes of Charmian and Iras?
3. Why does Antony go back to Rome?
4. To what line of Egyptian rulers does Cleopatra belong?
5. What gem does Antony kiss and send Cleopatra as a parting gift?
6. What famous man does Cleopatra recall as having loved in her younger days?

7. What does Agrippa suggest as a means of holding the bickering triumvirs together?
8. On what river did Antony and Cleopatra first meet?
9. Who, in speaking of Cleopatra, says: "Age cannot wither her, nor custom stale Her infinite variety"?
10. When Cleopatra beats a messenger, pulls his hair and draws a knife on him for telling her Antony is married to Octavia, what does the poor boy protest?
11. Who is carried out drunk from Pompey's banquet?
12. How does the messenger who was so badly beaten get into Cleopatra's good graces?
13. Under what pretext does Antony agree that Octavia go back to Rome?
14. What reason does Octavius give Antony for dismissing Lepidus from the triumvirate?
15. Which faithful follower of Antony deserts him and dies broken-hearted?
16. Who says the line: "I am dying, Egypt, dying"?
17. Which of the lovers dies first?
18. What is in the basket that conceals the asp?
19. Besides Cleopatra, does anyone else die from the bite of the asp?
20. Who now controls the Roman Empire?

69. TITUS ANDRONICUS

1. From what wars does Titus return victorious after ten years of fighting?
2. Who is offered as a sacrifice to appease the souls of the dead sons of Titus?
3. At whose recommendation is Saturninus made Emperor?
4. Why is Lavania forced to reject Saturninus' proposal of marriage?

5. Why does Titus kill his son, Mutius?

6. How soon does Saturninus marry Tamora?

7. What effect does the death of Alarbus have on Tamora?

8. Name the two villains who kill Bassianus.

9. Which two men are trapped and made to appear as if they were the murderers of Bassianus?

10. What mayhem do Tamora's two sons inflict on Lavinia?

11. Who compares Lavinia to Philomel?

12. How had Philomel exposed her mutilators?

13. What does Titus send to the Emperor in the belief that he is ransoming his two sons?

14. What book does Lavinia succeed in bringing to the notice of her family?

15. How does Lavinia inform her father who her mutilators are?

16. To whom does Titus address messages that are fastened to arrows and shot into the Emperor's courtyard?

17. With whom does Aemilius compare Lucius when he leads the Goths against Rome?

18. How is Titus dressed when he appears at his own banquet?

19. How many people are stabbed to death at the banquet?

20. Who is hailed as the new Emperor of Rome?

"TO PLAY A
PLEASANT COMEDY"

(The Taming of the Shrew)

70. *AS YOU LIKE IT*

1. In which country does this play seemingly take place?
2. What has Orlando been taught to do by his guardian brother?
3. At what event do Rosalind and Orlando first meet and fall in love?
4. Why does Frederick's admiration for Orlando change to hate?
5. What does Rosalind give to Orlando, apologizing that due to circumstances she cannot give him a better gift?
6. Who makes the philosophical statement that the "uses of adversity" are sweet?
7. When Rosalind and Celia leave home, whom do they take with them for protection?
8. When Orlando first finds the elder Duke and his companions in the Forest of Arden, what uncivil thing does he do?
9. Who delivers the dissertation on the Seven Ages of Man?
10. Why does Oliver go to the Forest?
11. Where do Rosalind and Celia live in the woods?

12. How does Celia recognize Orlando?

13. Quote the line in the third act that appears also in Marlowe's *Hero and Leander*.

14. What incident brings about Oliver's repentance for his treatment of Orlando?

15. What unmanly weakness does male-attired Rosalind show when she learns that Orlando has been wounded?

16. Who falls madly in love with Rosalind, mistaking her for a man?

17. Give the line that three characters repeat word for word in succession.

18. Who calls the girl he loves "an ill-favoured thing"?

19. Name the character who makes his first and only entrance in the last scene, bringing news of Duke Frederick's conversion.

20. Who performs the wedding ceremony?

71. *THE COMEDY OF ERRORS*

1. Why has Aegeon been arrested and condemned to die at sundown?

2. What was the only way the two Antipholuses could be distinguished from each other when they were babies?

3. How did the two Antipholuses happen to be the masters of the two Dromios?

4. Which of the Antipholuses was born first?

5. Why did Aegeon come to Ephesus?

6. Who would save Aegeon from death if he could do so with impunity?

7. What is the name of the inn where Antipholus of Syracuse is stopping?

8. What is the name of the house in which Adriana, Luciana, and Antipholus of Ephesus live?

9. What item of jewelry has Antipholus of Ephesus commissioned Angelo to make for him?
10. When Antipholus of Ephesus brings Angelo and Balthazar home to dinner, what welcome does he get?
11. When Luciana thinks she is talking to her sister's husband, what advice does she give him about infidelity?
12. What is the name of the wife of Dromio of Ephesus?
13. Why does Dromio of Syracuse think Dowsabel is a witch?
14. What country does Antipholus of Syracuse refer to as the land of sorcerers?
15. According to Dromio of Syracuse what kind of spoon should a person have if he "must eat with the devil"?
16. Where do Antipholus of Syracuse and his Dromio go to escape the wrath of Adriana when she insists on having them both bound?
17. Who gives Adriana a good lecture on jealousy?
18. How old are both sets of twins at the time of the play?
19. How do Antipholus of Ephesus and his Dromio free themselves when they are left tied up in a dark, damp room?
20. How is Aegeon's life saved?

72. LOVE'S LABOUR'S LOST

1. For how long do the King and the gentlemen of his court swear to do nothing but study?
2. What regulations are placed on their eating habits?
3. How is sleep to be controlled?
4. When the King makes the law that no one is to be seen talking to a woman, what has he forgotten?
5. Name the man who entertains the recluses with curious tales; the King admits he loves to hear him lie.
6. When Armado calls Moth a "tender juvenal," what does Moth call him?

7. What is Constable Dull's first name?

8. Who is ordered by the King to be taken into custody for a week with a diet of bran and water for being seen with a girl?

9. Who is the first to confess he is in love?

10. Where did Biron and Rosaline once dance together?

11. Why does the Princess of France come to see the King of Navarre?

12. The title to which French province is under consideration in the negotiations?

13. Why is Costard allowed to come out of jail?

14. How do the young French ladies while away the time?

15. Being illiterate, whom does Jaquenetta have read the letter which was meant for Rosaline but given to her by Costard in error?

16. How many of the men break their pledges?

17. What does Longaville call Maria, which he points out was not included in the oath, and therefore he is not breaking the oath?

18. How do the men justify breaking their pledges?

19. What news from France breaks up the entertainment that is being presented?

20. Before the ladies leave for France, what length of time do they stipulate for their lovers to wait for them?

73. *THE MERRY WIVES OF WINDSOR*

1. What are the charges against Falstaff and his comrades that Justice Shallow intends to make a Star-chamber matter of?

2. What are the given names of Shallow and Slender?

3. What position does the Host of the Garter Inn give Bardolph?

4. Why does Sir John Falstaff play up to the two Merry Wives?
5. Identify the three men who are bent on marrying Anne Page.
6. What does Mistress Quickly think is John Rugby's worst fault?
7. Why does Doctor Caius challenge Sir Hugh Evans to a duel?
8. What do Mistress Ford and Mistress Page discover about the letters Falstaff has written them?
9. Which of the two husbands is the jealous one?
10. On what occasion does Pistol say: "Why, then the world's mine oyster, which I with sword will open"?
11. Who exclaims intermittently, "O sweet Anne Page!"?
12. Who, according to the Host of the Garter, capers, dances, has eyes of youth, writes verses, "speaks holiday," and "smells April and May"?
13. Why does Page object to Fenton as a son-in-law?
14. Who promises all three of Anne's suitors to promote their courtships but is partial to Fenton?
15. How does Falstaff escape from the Ford house without being discovered by Ford?
16. What does Mistress Page declare wives may be, even if they are merry?
17. What legendary huntsman does Falstaff impersonate in Windsor Park?
18. When Falstaff thinks that, at long last, he is going to make love to the Merry Wives, what does he say the sky can rain?
19. When Slender thinks he is eloping with Anne, who does it turn out to be?
20. What does Doctor Caius have to report when he returns from his elopement?

74. *A MIDSUMMER-NIGHT'S DREAM*

1. Whose wedding is to take place in four days?
2. What two alternatives is Hermia given if she refuses to marry Demetrius?
3. Why does Helena tell Demetrius that Hermia and Lysander are eloping?
4. What is the name of the play the six craftsmen plan to perform for the wedding?
5. Who is author and director of the play?
6. Who wants to act all the parts in the little drama?
7. What pair is "Ill met by moonlight"?
8. For what reason does Puck "put a girdle round about the earth In forty minutes"?
9. Why does Oberon want to enchant Titania's eyes?
10. Why does Puck mistake Lysander for Demetrius?
11. Who is so transparent that Lysander (with drops in his eyes) can see her heart through her bosom?
12. Why does Bottom want a calendar and an almanac?
13. Who fixes the ass's head on Bottom?
14. What do Demetrius and Hermia accuse each other of doing with Lysander?
15. How many characters are enchanted with the drops?
16. How does Puck restore Lysander's love for Hermia?
17. What particular physical annoyance does Bottom suffer while he has an ass's head?
18. What two foods does Bottom ask the players not to eat?
19. What does the man "with lanthorn, dog, and bush of thorn" present?
20. Which character in the playlet sees a voice and hears a face?

75. THE TAMING OF THE SHREW

1. Who acts the part of Christopher Sly's wife when he is being persuaded to believe he is a married man?
2. When arrangements are being made for Sly's entertainment, what does his host recommend to the Page that will help him shed tears?
3. Why does Baptista discourage all suitors for Bianca's hand?
4. Who changes clothes with his servant so he can pose as Bianca's tutor?
5. What does Sly think of this play that is being presented for his benefit?
6. Why has Petruchio left Verona and come to Padua?
7. What men are delighted that Petruchio is willing to marry Katharina?
8. Why does Katharina tie her sister's hands and strike her?
9. When Baptista is asked by Petruchio if he has "a daughter, Call'd Katharina, fair and virtuous," what does he answer?
10. Why does Katharina hit Hortensio with a lute?
11. Which of Bianca's suitors is an old gray-haired man?
12. Why does Katharina weep on her wedding day?
13. Who gives a graphic picture of Petruchio's ridiculous costume before he arrives?
14. When the Priest asks Petruchio if he will take Katharina for his wife, what does he answer?
15. What important pair is missing at the wedding feast?
16. In which season of the year does this wedding take place?
17. What kind of meat is served but not tasted by the newly wedded pair at Petruchio's house?
18. Under what circumstances does Petruchio make the speech containing the line: "For 'tis the mind that makes the body rich"?

19. Whom is Petruchio describing to Katharina when he says, "Hast thou beheld a fresher gentlewoman? Such war of white and red within her cheeks"?
20. How does Petruchio prove that he has tamed the shrew?

76. THE TEMPEST

1. Why is the storm raging?
2. What is the only thing Miranda remembers about her life before she came to the island?
3. How long have Prospero and Miranda been on the island?
4. Who helped Antonio usurp Prospero's dukedom?
5. What benevolent man put necessary provisions in the little boat when Prospero and his daughter were set adrift?
6. What does Prospero prize above his dukedom?
7. Why did Prospero turn against Caliban after years of friendship?
8. Who taught Caliban how to speak?
9. How is Ferdinand led to Miranda?
10. What does Prospero promise Ariel for carrying out his orders?
11. Name the two men who plot to kill Alonso while he is sleeping?
12. What country is Trinculo referring to when he says, "any strange beast there makes a man"?
13. Who keeps Prospero informed about everything that is taking place in the different parts of the island?
14. What hard work does Prospero give Ferdinand to do?
15. Name the three characters who plot to kill Prospero and take over the island.
16. What happens to the fine banquet Ariel puts before the hungry King and Duke?

17. Why is the celebration of the betrothal of Ferdinand and Miranda interrupted?
18. Identify Mountain, Fury, Silver, and Tyrant.
19. Where does Ariel plan to live "merrily," now that he has his freedom?
20. What does Miranda call the land she is going to that has such wonderful people in it?

77. TWELFTH NIGHT

1. How were Viola and Sebastian separated?
2. As what sort of person does Viola suggest to the Captain that she have herself introduced to Duke Orsino?
3. Who is drunk every night with drinking to Olivia's health?
4. What do Olivia and Viola have in common?
5. Who loves Olivia "With adorations, fertile tears, With groans that thunder love, with sighs of fire"?
6. To whom does Viola make her beautiful "willow cabin" speech?
7. What was the name of the father of the twins?
8. Who has many enemies at Orsino's court, but is willing to brave the dangers for Sebastian's sake?
9. Why do the members of Olivia's household want Malvolio out of the way?
10. How is the letter meant for Malvolio delivered to him?
11. What three things does the letter tell Malvolio he is to do to win Olivia?
12. Sir Toby tells Maria to write as many lies as she can get on a sheet big enough for a certain bed. What famous bed is it?
13. What is the name of the inn where Sebastian and Antonio are staying?

14. Name the two characters who are tricked into fighting a duel.
15. Who interrupts the duel thinking Viola is Sebastian?
16. When does Viola first get an inkling that her brother is still alive?
17. Does Olivia know whom she is calling "husband"?
18. What does Viola remember about her father, which proves to Sebastian that she is his sister?
19. Who says: "How now, Malvolio!"?
20. On whom does Malvolio vow vengeance?

78. THE TWO GENTLEMEN OF VERONA

1. What sort of wits does Valentine contend home-keeping youths have?
2. Where does Valentine go "To see the wonders of the world abroad"?
3. Who has "metamorphosed" Proteus?
4. Why does Julia tear up the letter Proteus sends her?
5. What relation are Proteus and Valentine to each other?
6. Who is the first to discover that Valentine is in love?
7. What does Speed say is the reason Valentine cannot see Silvia if he loves her?
8. When Silvia asks Valentine to write a letter to a friend for her, who does the friend turn out to be?
9. What is the name of Launce's Dog?
10. Who is the Duke of Milan's choice for the hand of Silvia?
11. What happens to Proteus' love for Julia as soon as he sees Silvia?
12. When Valentine and Silvia plan to elope, who squeals on them to her father?
13. How does the Duke trick Valentine into making his plot quite obvious?

14. How does Proteus get permission to visit Silvia in her tower?
15. What lie does Valentine tell the outlaws, to get into their good graces?
16. Who sings the song, "Who is Silvia?"
17. Are Sir Eglamour, Julia's suitor, and Sir Eglamour, Silvia's agent, the same person?
18. What great sacrifice is Launce willing to make for his master when the dog, which Proteus ordered him to take to Silvia, is stolen?
19. Who proves himself a coward when he is challenged to fight for the girl he loves?
20. How does Valentine repay the outlaws for their loyalty and service to him?

"VERY TRAGICAL MIRTH"

(A Midsummer-Night's Dream)

79. ALL'S WELL THAT ENDS WELL

1. What is the name of the noted physician who died six months ago?
2. Who has taken the doctor's daughter into her home as a gentlewoman?
3. What is the ailment of the King of France that the deceased doctor could have cured?
4. To whom is Helena speaking when she first admits she is in love with Bertram?
5. To whom is Helena referring when she says: "I know him a notorious liar, Think him a great way fool, solely a coward"?
6. What Italians are fighting each other in an undecided war?
7. What reason does Helena give the Countess for following Bertram to Paris?
8. Who introduces Helena to the King of France?
9. What reward does Helena ask if she succeeds in curing the King?
10. In what length of time does Helena effect the cure?
11. How does Bertram react when Helena chooses him?
12. Bertram writes Helena that she cannot call him husband until two things happen. What are they?

13. Where does Bertram go immediately after the wedding?
14. What feminine character appears briefly in this play but does not utter a word?
15. How is Helena disguised when she arrives in Florence?
16. What news does Bertram receive that makes him decide to go back to France?
17. What is Bertram wearing when he returns home that baffles the King and Bertram himself?
18. Why is Bertram arrested?
19. How does Helena manage to comply with the terms of Bertram's letter?
20. Who says "ALL'S WELL THAT ENDS WELL."

80. MEASURE FOR MEASURE

1. Whom does Duke Vincentio appoint ruler during his absence?
2. Whose type of peace do the citizens of Vienna definitely not want?
3. Why does Vincentio disguise himself as a friar and stay in Vienna?
4. Why has Claudio been arrested and doomed to lose his head?
5. Who is the only person that knows Vincentio is still in Vienna?
6. Where is the Duke supposed to have gone?
7. Why does Francisca send Isabella to speak to Lucio when he comes to the nunnery?
8. Whose blood is "very snow-broth"?
9. Name the character who brings before Angelo "two notorious benefactors"?
10. What is Froth accused of eating all but two of, that Elbow's pregnant wife craves?

11. When Isabella is pleading before Angelo for her brother's life, who spurs her on and tells her how she is doing?

12. What price does Angelo ask of Isabella for sparing her brother's life?

13. Who eavesdrops on Isabella when she tells Claudio of Angelo's perfidy?

14. Why has Angelo jilted Mariana?

15. What does Vincentio tell Isabella to do to save her brother's life, her own honor, Mariana's heart and Angelo's duty?

16. Where does "dejected Mariana" reside?

17. Who slanders the disguised Duke to his face?

18. Why does Pompey feel so much at home in prison?

19. What does Isabella instruct Mariana to say to Angelo when she leaves him?

20. Who says "MEASURE still for MEASURE"?

81. THE MERCHANT OF VENICE

1. Why does Bassanio want to borrow money from Antonio when he is already in debt to him?

2. How do we know Portia is a blonde?

3. For what reason is Portia's husband selected by the casket method?

4. When Portia says: "God made him, and therefore let him pass for a man," to whom is she referring?

5. Does anyone know, before the selecting starts, which is the right casket?

6. Do any of the suitors leave without choosing a casket?

7. How many of the suitors appear in the play?

8. From whom does Shylock say he will borrow money to lend to Antonio so that Antonio can lend it to Bassanio?

9. Is Antonio to pay any interest on the money Shylock lends him?

10. Why is Bassanio's dinner and masque called off?
11. How are the suitors to know if they choose the right casket?
12. What three oaths must each of the suitors take before he is permitted to make a choice?
13. What picture is in the silver casket?
14. What runaway is Tubal sent to look for?
15. What news disturbs the happiness of Portia and Bassanio?
16. Why does Portia insist on an immediate marriage?
17. Where do Nerissa and Portia pretend to go when they leave for Venice?
18. Who heckles Shylock during his trial?
19. What does Portia ask of Antonio as a remembrance rather than a fee?
20. Do the men or the women arrive at Portia's house first?

82. MUCH ADO ABOUT NOTHING

1. What young soldier "hath indeed better bettered expectation" and is especially cited for bravery by Don Pedro?
2. When Leonato says: "there are no faces truer than those that are so washed," how are they washed?
3. What does Beatrice sarcastically promise to do to all the men that Benedick has killed in battle?
4. The sight of whom renders Beatrice "heart-burned an hour after"?
5. Of all the insulting names that Beatrice calls Benedick, which one infuriates him most?
6. Who, pretending he thinks Claudio is Benedick, tells Claudio that Don Pedro wants Hero for himself?
7. Who proposes the subtle plan to Don John that will "vex Claudio," "undo Hero, and kill Leonato"?
8. What feat does Don Pedro liken to one of Hercules' labors?

9. About whose singing does Benedick remark, "An he had been a dog that should have howled thus, they would have hanged him"?

10. What do the friends of Beatrice and Benedick make of them to get them to fall in love with each other?

11. When Benedick finds himself falling in love with Beatrice, how does he explain his oath to die a bachelor?

12. What does Benedick say is the reason for his change in temperament?

13. Why are Hugh Oatcake and George Seacoal considered better fitted to be constable than the other men of the Watch?

14. How do the men of the Watch learn about the scene that has been enacted to mislead Claudio and Don Pedro?

15. What logical advice does Dogberry give his men concerning the most peaceable way to handle a thief?

16. Who innocently impersonates Hero at her window and compromises her?

17. What does Margaret recommend to Beatrice as the only cure for a qualm?

18. What does Friar Francis suggest as a means of clearing Hero's name?

19. What does Beatrice ask Benedick to do to prove his love for her?

20. Who finally convinces Claudio and Don Pedro that they have been duped?

83. THE WINTER'S TALE

1. Who is "an unspeakable comfort" to Leontes' subjects?
2. How long has Polixenes been a visitor in Sicilia?
3. What has suddenly made Leontes insanely jealous of Polixenes?

4. Who warns Polixenes that his life is in danger and leaves for Bohemia with him?
5. Who says, "A sad tale's best for winter"?
6. Where is the new little Princess born?
7. Whom does Leontes blame for the illness of Mamillius?
8. Who is given the cruel task of leaving the Princess exposed to the elements?
9. To what deity are Cleomenes and Dion sent?
10. When does Leontes first repent of his evil and confess his sins?
11. Who is the only person that is not afraid to tell the King what a blundering tyrant he is?
12. How does the Princess happen to be called Perdita?
13. Where does Antigonus leave the baby?
14. How does Antigonus meet his death?
15. Who brings up Perdita as his own child?
16. Who develops a case of nostalgia?
17. How do Florizel and Perdita happen to meet?
18. How long has Hermione vowed to remain dead to her husband?
19. What does Leontes notice about Hermione's (supposed) statue that he cannot understand?
20. Whom does Leontes recommend as an honourable husband for Paulina?

"THIS WOFUL TRAGEDY"

(Henry VI, Part I)

84. KING LEAR

1. Name the husbands of Goneril and Regan.
2. Why does King Lear ask his three daughters to tell him how much they love him?
3. Who has been Lear's favorite daughter up to now?
4. Who vehemently defends Cordelia when she refuses to flatter her father as her sisters have done?
5. What is in the letter that Edmund pretends he does not want his father to see?
6. How old is the Earl of Kent?
7. Who is King Lear's godson?
8. From whom does Kent receive a letter which gives a ray of hope for Lear?
9. Under what conditions do Regan and Goneril agree to take their father in?
10. When Lear and his companions seek refuge from a raging storm in a hovel, whom do they find there?
11. After the Earl of Gloucester has been blinded, how does cruel Regan suggest he get to Dover?
12. Who is fatally wounded by servants for torturing Gloucester?

13. Is the unnamed gentleman Kent meets in Dover the same one he sends earlier with a message to Cordelia?
14. Which of Lear's sons-in-law is sympathetic to him throughout?
15. For whose love are Goneril and Regan bitter rivals?
16. How do the two mean sisters die?
17. What is the outcome of the battle between the French and the British?
18. Who mortally wounds Edmund?
19. Whom does King Lear kill before he dies?
20. Who is left to rule Britain?

85. MACBETH

1. What is the battle the witches refer to that is to be "fought and won"?
2. Why is Banquo puzzled about the sex of the witches?
3. What three prophecies do the witches make when they meet Macbeth and Banquo?
4. From whom did Macbeth inherit his title, Thane of Glamis?
5. Why does Macbeth doubt the witches at first?
6. To whom is Duncan referring when he says: "There's no art To find the mind's construction in the face"?
7. What title is given Malcolm by his father?
8. What pertinent information does Lady Macbeth ask of her husband as soon as she learns King Duncan is to be their guest?
9. What reason does Lady Macbeth give for not killing Duncan herself?
10. Who is the first to discover that Duncan has been murdered?

11. According to Donalbain what are in men's smiles?
12. Where is Macbeth crowned?
13. Why is Macbeth "cribb'd, confined, bound in To saucy doubts and fears"?
14. Where is Duncan buried?
15. In whose place does Banquo's ghost sit at the banquet table?
16. How does Macbeth propose to "make assurance double sure"?
17. What reassurance does Macbeth get from the apparitions of two children?
18. What particular information does Macbeth want from the witches on his second meeting with them?
19. Why does Malcolm besmirch his own character to Macduff when they meet in England?
20. What title, that has never been used in Scotland, does Malcolm bestow on his thanes and kinsmen?

86. HAMLET

1. Why is Denmark armed?
2. What does Laertes warn Ophelia Hamlet's interest in her is?
3. What is the substance of Ophelia's reply?
4. Does Hamlet admit to anyone that he is going to act like a mad man?
5. What does Hamlet say was thrifty about his mother's marriage so soon after his father's funeral?
6. What was the poison that Claudius poured into his brother's ear?
7. Is Hamlet's first soliloquy ("O, that this too too solid flesh would melt") given before or after he talks with his father's ghost?

8. Who makes the observation that there is a method in Hamlet's madness?

9. What direction is the wind when Hamlet knows "a hawk from a handsaw"?

10. What reason does the King give Polonius for sending Hamlet to England?

11. Does Gertrude know that Claudius murdered his brother?

12. What is it "the lady doth protest too much," according to Gertrude?

13. How does Hamlet know someone is hiding behind the arras in his mother's room?

14. Whom does Hamlet think he is stabbing?

15. Why does the ghost appear to Hamlet the second time?

16. Who is Hamlet's closest friend and confidant?

17. What historical event took place the day Hamlet was born?

18. How old is Hamlet?

19. In what unsuitable place do Hamlet and Laertes fight about which of them loved Ophelia more?

20. How many members of the Danish royal family are alive when the play ends?

87. ROMEO AND JULIET

1. Who breaks up the servants brawl that starts the play?

2. When old Capulet shouts for a sword, what does his wife think is more appropriate?

3. How does Romeo learn that Rosaline is to attend the feast given by the Capulets?

4. Does Romeo say, "Here's much to do with hate, but more with love," before or after he meets Juliet?

5. How does Tybalt recognize Romeo in his mask at the ball?

6. Whom has Juliet's family selected for her to marry?

7. Why does Juliet ask Romeo not to swear by the moon?

8. Who does the actual proposing? Romeo or Juliet?

9. What happens to Romeo's love for Rosaline?

10. Which two characters definitely know that Romeo and Juliet are married?

11. What effect does the Friar sincerely hope the marriage will have?

12. How does Romeo hope to improve matters when he threatens to use a dagger on himself?

13. What two birds do Romeo and Juliet argue about the last time they see each other alive?

14. When Juliet is pining her heart away for Romeo, what does her family think is the cause of her grief?

15. How much time is Juliet given to prepare for her wedding with Paris?

16. What name is used in such a way that it might refer to either the Nurse or Lady Capulet?

17. Why isn't Friar Laurence's message delivered to Romeo in Mantua?

18. Who kills Paris?

19. How does Romeo die?

20. How does Juliet die?

88. OTHELLO

1. Why does Iago turn against Othello?

2. What is Cassio's first name?

3. Against whom does the Duke command Othello to lead the Venetian troops?

4. Who says Othello's story would win *his* daughter too?

5. How old is Iago?

6. By what deceptive nickname is Iago called?

7. How does Iago persuade Roderigo that he should kill Cassio?
8. With whom does Iago suspect Emilia of having been unfaithful to him?
9. What people does Iago say are "most potent in potting"?
10. Who is wounded by Cassio in the brawl the night of the victory celebration?
11. What kind of music does the Clown tell the musicians Othello would like them to play?
12. What is the decoration on the fatal handkerchief?
13. Who replaces Cassio as Othello's Lieutenant?
14. Who is supposed to have made the handkerchief?
15. Who is in possession of the handkerchief when **Othello** sees it the first time after it has disappeared?
16. Who is the last person to be in possession of the handkerchief?
17. What saves Cassio from being mortally wounded when he is attacked by Roderigo?
18. After Othello smothers Desdemona what does Emilia call their marriage?
19. Othello having been relieved of his command, who is made governor of Cyprus?
20. Who inherits Othello's estate after his death?

"THIS STRANGE
EVENTFUL HISTORY"

(As You Like It)

89. KING JOHN

1. Whom do the French consider the rightful heir to the throne of England?
2. Who was John's noted brother, often mentioned in the play?
3. Who is knighted by John and given the title of Sir Richard Plantagenet?
4. Who is John's principal confident and mainstay?
5. Why does the Duke of Austria join in the war?
6. Although Chatillon leaves for France ahead of John, how does it happen they arrive the same day?
7. What two women argue so bitterly that Prince Arthur weeps and wishes he were dead?
8. How does Queen Elinor propose to prove John's right to the English throne?
9. What English-held city refuses to open its gates until the succession to the throne is established?
10. What marriage is agreed upon that brings about a temporary truce?

11. Which character furnishes the very clever comedy for this play?
12. Who is Pope at this time?
13. Whom does the Pope wish installed as Archbishop of Canterbury?
14. Who incites King Philip to break his treaty with King John?
15. How does John get the money to continue the war?
16. Who is ordered to burn Arthur's eyes out?
17. What evil omen is reported to have been seen in the sky by many people when the report of Arthur's death is spread?
18. On whom does the Dauphin put the blame for his invasion of England?
19. At whose request does King John forgive the English lords who joined with the French?
20. Who poisons King John?

90. RICHARD II

1. Whose recent death makes the members of the royal family suspicious of one another?
2. Why does Richard reduce Bolingbroke's exile from ten to six years?
3. Why does Richard want John of Gaunt to die quickly?
4. Why is Richard unpopular?
5. Where does Bolingbroke land when he returns from France?
6. Whom does Bolingbroke greet with, "I count myself in nothing else so happy As in a soul remembering my good friends"?
7. What infirmity prevents the Duke of York from chastising his nephew for his treason?

8. Name the two companions of Richard that Bolingbroke orders beheaded.

9. What compromise is Bolingbroke willing to make with Richard?

10. What does the distracted Queen wish her gardener because he tells her the King is captured?

11. At the last meeting with his Queen what does Richard recommend that she do after she is deported to France?

12. Who is discovered by his father to be part of a plot to murder Bolingbroke?

13. When the Duke of Aumerle is demoted, what title is he given?

14. Where does Bolingbroke suggest that his wayward son might be found?

15. Where is Richard imprisoned?

16. Who is the only friend that visits Richard in prison?

17. What is the name of Richard's horse that Bolingbroke rides to his coronation?

18. Why does Richard suspect that he is to be murdered?

19. What clergyman is executed as a conspirator against the new King?

20. How is the news of Richard's murder brought to the King?

91. HENRY IV, PART I

1. For what reason does Henry plan an expedition to the Holy Land?

2. Who is the leader of the bloody revolt in Wales?

3. Name the brave young man who put down the uprising in Scotland.

4. Who is the only prisoner that Hotspur is willing to relinquish to the King?

5. What is Falstaff's favorite drink?
6. What position does the Prince of Wales jokingly promise Falstaff?
7. How does Prince Henry rationalize about his iniquities?
8. Who, before his death, had proclaimed Edmund Mortimer heir to the English throne?
9. What two steps does Hotspur threaten to take after the King forbids him to mention Mortimer again?
10. What trick do the Prince and Poins play on Falstaff?
11. Who receives and reads a letter aloud, but never lets the audience know who wrote it?
12. What is the motto of the Percy family?
13. Who considers himself blessed with supernatural powers because of strange phenomena at the time of his birth?
14. The absence of what two allies weakens Hotspur's cause?
15. Who accepts bribes from the best soldiers in his command for their freedom?
16. What does King Henry accuse Worcester of proclaiming at market-crosses and reading in churches?
17. Who might have stopped the fighting if he had not withheld from Hotspur, King Henry's liberal peace terms?
18. Who, in the King's apparel and claiming to be the King, is killed by Douglas?
19. On what occasion does Falstaff assert, "The better part of valour is discretion"?
20. What battle is fought at the end of this play?

92. HENRY IV, PART II

1. What does Rumour have as decoration on his costume?
2. What news would have made Northumberland sick if he had been well but it makes him well since he is sick?

3. Name the two men who lead the King's army against the revolt of Northumberland.

4. To whom did the Prince of Wales once give a box on the ear?

5. What is the ailment of the King?

6. What does Falstaff answer when the Chief Justice accuses him of leading the Prince astray?

7. What church dignitary is the Crown's most formidable adversary?

8. Why does Prince Henry refrain from showing his sincere grief that his father is ill?

9. Whom is Prince Henry ridiculously reported to be engaged to marry?

10. What imperfection in Hotspur does Lady Percy say "nature made his blemish"?

11. Name the "swaggering" follower of Falstaff introduced in this play.

12. Under what circumstances does Prince Henry hear Falstaff make disparaging remarks about him?

13. Whom has Mistress Quickly known for twenty-nine years, "come peascod-time"?

14. What is the familiar last line of King Henry's soliloquy on his insomnia?

15. What does Prince John do after promising Scroop and his corebels that all their grievances will be redressed if they will disband and surrender their arms?

16. Which of Prince Henry's brothers is his favorite, according to the King?

17. What is the fate of the Earl of Northumberland?

18. What substitute is given the King for his pilgrimage to the Holy Land?

19. Why is the Lord Chief Justice dubious about his position after Henry V becomes King?

20. Who suffers most by the new King's reformation?

93. HENRY V

1. What ancient law has been revived to try to keep Henry from the throne of France?
2. Who convinces Henry that the French have ignored this law, so he can too?
3. What gift does the Dauphin send derisively to Henry in answer to his claim of a few dukedoms?
4. Whom does Mistress Quickly jilt when she marries Pistol?
5. Who dies utterly forlorn because Henry has discarded him?
6. Who is spokesman for Henry at the French court and demands that King Charles give up his crown to Henry's just claim?
7. Who desires "Nothing but odds with England"?
8. What does King Charles offer Henry to appease him?
9. During which siege does Henry make the magnificent speech that begins, "Once more unto the breach, dear friends, once more"?
10. Which English soldier will not say his prayers for fear people would think him a coward?
11. Which of the former followers of Falstaff is executed for robbing a church?
12. What clothing accessory is mentioned seventeen times in one act?
13. What is the decisive battle in this war?
14. From whom does Henry borrow a cloak to disguise himself?
15. For what deceased King does Henry have continual masses sung?
16. On what special day does the battle of Agincourt take place?
17. Name the French herald who comes twice to offer peace

terms to Henry and a third time for permission to count the dead and bury them.

18. Who discourses on Alexander the Great, comparing Henry to him?
19. Who is forced to eat leek?
20. According to the Epilogue, why does Henry VI lose France?

94. HENRY VI, PART I

1. At what sad event do three messengers come to Westminster Abbey with news of rebellions in France?
2. Whom do the English consider the rightful King of France when Henry VI becomes King of England?
3. Who, in his thoughts, musters an army that overruns France?
4. Name the coward who runs away and leaves Lord Talbot to be captured.
5. Who leads the English while Talbot is prisoner?
6. Who brings Joan of Arc to the Dauphin?
7. What is the first thing Charles does to convince himself that Joan has mystical powers?
8. What does an English soldier cry out before Orleans that causes the French to flee and leave him many spoils?
9. When does Charles call Joan a "deceitful dame"?
10. What Frenchman fights on the side of the English?
11. Name the woman who wants to become famous by trapping Talbot in her castle.
12. Who is William de la Pole?
13. What strong claimant to the English throne dies at this time in the Tower of London after years of imprisonment?
14. How is Joan disguised when she enters the gates of Rouen?

15. To whom does Joan say, "One drop of blood drawn from thy country's bosom Should grieve thee more than streams of foreign gore"?
16. Where do Talbot and King Henry meet for the first time?
17. Who puts the crown of France on Henry's head in Paris?
18. Who captures Joan?
19. Why does the Earl of Suffolk promote the marriage of Margaret and King Henry?
20. What titles does Reignier, Margaret's father, hold?

95. HENRY VI, PART II

1. What is extraordinary about Henry's marriage to Margaret?
2. What duchies are forfeited to Reignier in the marriage contract?
3. What title does Henry bestow on the Earl of Suffolk for bringing him such a lovely queen?
4. Who does Gloucester say now "rules the roast"?
5. Who had fought hard to win the lost duchies and weeps when he learns they are gone?
6. Who pledges to himself that he will seize the throne of England and perfume the air with the white rose?
7. Identify the two men who hire John Hume to betray the Duchess of Gloucester.
8. Why does Queen Margaret give the Duchess a box on the ear?
9. How does Saunder Simpcox give himself away when he pretends he has been blind all his life except for the last half hour?
10. In case of Henry's death at this time, who is next in line for the throne?

11. At the Duke of Gloucester's treason trial, who is the only person to say a kind word in his behalf?

12. Whom does the Duke of York hire to make trouble at home while he goes to Ireland, superficially to put down a rebellion?

13. To whom is the Earl of Warwick referring when he says, "So bad a death argues a monstrous life"?

14. How does the Duke of Suffolk meet his end?

15. What does Dick the Butcher suggest, the first thing he and Cade's men should do when they come to power?

16. How old was Henry when he became King?

17. Who kills Cade?

18. What lie does the Duke of Buckingham tell the Duke of York to get him to disband his Irish army?

19. Who is the first to mention the deformity of York's son Richard?

20. Whose life does Richard save three times at the battle of St. Alban's.

96. HENRY VI, PART III

1. When Henry arrives at the Parliament-house where does he find the Duke of York?

2. What concession is Henry required to make in order to retain his crown?

3. What sort of crown does Queen Margaret place on the Duke of York's head?

4. Who cruelly murders the Earl of Rutland and helps Margaret stab the Duke of York?

5. Whose head replaces the Duke of York's on York gates?

6. Which son of the Duke of York inherits his title?

7. Who has become the "setter up and plucker down of kings"?

8. When Edward IV becomes King what unwanted title does he bestow on his brother Richard?
9. How does Warwick happen to be at the French court at the same time as Queen Margaret?
10. What news is brought to France that turns Warwick against King Edward?
11. With whom is a marriage arranged for the Prince of Wales by mutual consent of Margaret and Warwick?
12. What familiar title is Lady Grey given after her marriage to Edward?
13. Who marries Warwick's younger daughter?
14. In what battle is Warwick killed?
15. At whose hands does Prince Edward die?
16. When Margaret asks the murderers to kill her too, who offers to do it?
17. Where do King Henry and the Earl of Richmond meet for the first time?
18. What is the sad end of Henry VI.
19. Who helps Margaret get back to France?
20. How fares King Edward IV at the end of the play?

97. RICHARD III

1. There is a prophecy that the issue of Edward IV will be disinherited by a member of his family, whose name begins with a certain letter. What letter is it?
2. What reason is given the Duke of Clarence for his imprisonment in the Tower?
3. Who berates Richard most bitingly and spits at him before the coffin of Henry VI?
4. What is the relationship of the Earl of Richmond and Lord Stanley?
5. What woman appears with prophesies and curses?

6. On whom does Richard try to lay the blame for most of his villainy?

7. Prince Edward recalls the man who began the building of the Tower of London. Who was he?

8. What two women does Richard accuse of practicing witchcraft and marking him with a withered arm?

9. Who is Mistress Shore's protector after the death of Edward IV?

10. Why is Hastings beheaded?

11. How does Richard go about discrediting Edward IV and his sons?

12. Who helps Richard put on an act in which, for the benefit of the Lord Mayor of London, he pretends he does not want the throne?

13. How much of the play has elapsed before Richard is crowned King?

14. What rumor does Richard order Sir William Catesby to spread concerning Queen Anne?

15. Whom does Richard hire to kill the Princes in the Tower?

16. What causes Buckingham to turn against Richard?

17. Whom has Richard selected for his second wife?

18. Whose son does Richard hold as hostage?

19. Where do Richard and Richmond meet to fight it out?

20. Richmond's coming marriage to what Princess is announced by him?

98. HENRY VIII

1. Identify the two "suns of glory" who met in the vale of Andren for the costly festivities held there.

2. Who originated this extravagant show of splendor?

3. What illness did the Duke of Buckingham suffer that kept him from attending these festivities?

4. At the meeting in the council-chamber in London, who petitions the King about the taxation caused by the extravagances of Cardinal Wolsey?

5. On whose evidence is Buckingham convicted of treason?

6. What relative of Buckingham's does Wolsey send to Ireland to prevent him from aiding the Duke?

7. Where does King Henry first become enamored of Anne Bullen?

8. What does the Duke of Norfolk answer when the Lord Chamberlain tells him the King's marriage "Has crept too near his conscience"?

9. What title does the King bestow on Anne Bullen?

10. After the King divorces Katharine, what title does *she* have?

11. Whom does Wolsey plan for the King to marry?

12. Why is the Cardinal against Henry's marriage to Anne?

13. What papers that are meant for the Pope fall into Henry's hands and ruin Wolsey?

14. Who is chosen to take Wolsey's place as Lord Chancellor?

15. What is the technicality used to force the divorce on Katharine?

16. Where does Cardinal Wolsey die?

17. Who gives so generous an account of Wolsey's good deeds, that Katharine would like him for her own chronicler?

18. Where does Katharine end her days?

19. What card game do Henry VIII and the Duke of Suffolk play the night Princess Elizabeth is born?

20. Whom does the King name godfather to his new daughter?

(*Julius Caesar*)

PART IV

"The End of This Day's Business"

99. "THE END OF THIS DAY'S BUSINESS" Number 1

Let's put an end to each of the following quotations by adding familiar expressions of two or more words.

1. Such enchanting presence and discourse
   Hath almost made me . . . .
2. Nor tripped neither, you base . . . -. . . . .
3. Let Hercules himself do what he may,
   The cat will mew, and . . . .
   . . .
4. Notwithstanding that, I know Anne's mind,—that's . . .-
   . . . .
5. What, all my pretty chickens and their dam
   . . . .
6. Most radiant, exquisite and unmatchable beauty,—I pray
   you, tell me if this be . . . .
7. O, that men's ears should be
   To counsel deaf, but . . . .
8. But yet you draw not iron, for my heart
   Is . . . .
9. This bird you aim'd at, though you hit her not;
   Therefore a health to all that . . . . ' .
10. 'Tis time to fear when tyrants . . . .
11. Good signiors both, when shall we laugh? . . . .
12. When in the why and the wherefore is . . . .
    . . . .
13. The hind that would be mated by the lion
    Must . . . .
14. Men have died from time to time and worms have eaten
    them, ...

15. A friend should bear . . . . ' . . . . . .–
. . . .

16. Some Cupid kills with arrows, ...
. . . . .

17.   The taste of sweetness, whereof a little
More than a little is by . . . .

18. O all you host of heaven! O earth! . . . .

19. Why then, can one desire . . . .
. . . .

20. Here will be an old abusing of God's patience and . . .
. . . . ' . . . .

100. "THE END OF THIS DAY'S BUSINESS"
Number 2

1. He was never yet a breaker of proverbs: he will . . . .
. . . .

2. Dost thou think, because thou art virtuous, there shall be
no more . . . .

3. What, man! more water glideth by the mill
Than . . . .

4. Out of their saddles into the dirt; . . . .
. . . .

5. Why, I, in this weak piping time of peace,
Have no delight to . . . .

6. It warms the very sickness in my heart,
That I shall live and . . . .

7. I hope it is no dishonest desire to desire to be . . . . . .
. . . .

8. It is for all, all I have. He hath . . . .
. . . .

9. Those that understood him smiled at one another and shook

their heads; but for mine own part, ...

. . . .

10. When Fortune means to men most good,
She looks upon them with . . . .

11. And I'll be sworn I have power to shame him hence.
O, while you live, ...

. . . .

12. Paris is dirt to him; and, I warrant, Helen, to change, would
give an eye . . . . . .

13. If he fall in, good night! or . . . .

14. O, my offence is rank, it . . . .

15. Dost thou conjure for wenches, that thou call'st for such
store,
When one is . . . .

16. Immortal gods, I crave no pelf;
I pray for . . . .

17. Therefore paucas pallabris; . . . .

. . . . .

18. That would hang us . . . . ' . . . . .

19. For every man hath business and desire,

. . . .

20. Society is no comfort
To . . . .

PART V

Answers

"SUNDRY
CONTEMPLATIONS"

1. "SUNDRY CONTEMPLATIONS"

1. Coriolanus.
2. Barnardine, in *Measure for Measure*.
3. Helena, in *All's Well That Ends Well*.
4. Pompey, in *Antony and Cleopatra*.
5. Jaques', in *As You Like It*.
6. Dromio of Ephesus, in *The Comedy of Errors*.
7. Queen Margaret, in *Henry VI, Part II*.
8. Cardinal Wolsey, in *Henry VIII*.
9. Anne Bullen, in *Henry VIII*.
10. The Dauphin Lewis, in *King John*.
11. Earl of Kent, disguised, in *King Lear*.
12. *Timon of Athens*.
13. Portia, in *The Merchant of Venice*.
14. The sailor-husband of the "rump-fed ronyon," in *Macbeth*.
15. Saturninus, in *Titus Andronicus*.
16. First fisherman, in *Pericles*.
17. Juliet, in *Romeo and Juliet*.
18. Gonzalo, in *The Tempest*.
19. The love of something new even though it is something old made over, in *Troilus and Cressida*.
20. *A Midsummer-Night's Dream*.

2. "SUNDRY CONTEMPLATIONS"

1. Elbow, in *Measure for Measure.*
2. Autolycus, in *The Winter's Tale.*
3. *Julius Caesar.*
4. Don Adriano de Armado, in *Love's Labour's Lost.*
5. In the Duke of Norfolk's description of the "earthly glory" in France, in *Henry VIII.*
6. First Witch, in *Macbeth.*
7. Lord Talbot, in *Henry VI, Part I.*
8. Earl of Salisbury and Earl of Warwick, in *Henry VI, Part II.*
9. Scotland, in *Henry V.*
10. Edward, Earl of March, in *Henry VI, Part III.*
11. Yes. Falstaff claims that she has been saying around town that her eldest son looks like the Chief Justice, in *Henry IV, Part II.*
12. Earl of Gloucester, in *King Lear.*
13. *Hamlet.*
14. Hotspur, in *Henry IV, Part I.*
15. Queen to *Cymbeline.*
16. Menenius Agrippa, in *Coriolanus.*
17. Aegeon, in *The Comedy of Errors.*
18. Octavius Caesar when Antony's sword is brought to him, in *Antony and Cleopatra.*
19. "A precious jewel," in *As You Like It.*
20. Rosalind, in *As You Like It.*

3. "SUNDRY CONTEMPLATIONS"

1. King Hamlet's Ghost is speaking of Gertrude, in *Hamlet.*
2. Coriolanus.

3. Octavia and Octavius, in *Antony and Cleopatra.*
4. Edmund Mortimer and his Welsh wife, in *Henry IV, Part I.*
5. Nurse to Juliet, in *Romeo and Juliet.*
6. *Henry V.*
7. Queen Margaret, in *Henry VI, Part II.*
8. Bishop of Winchester, in *Henry VI, Part I.*
9. Lavinia's, in *Titus Andronicus.*
10. Macbeth.
11. *Love's Labour's Lost.*
12. Slender, in *The Merry Wives of Windsor.*
13. Julius Caesar.
14. Hero, in *Much Ado About Nothing.*
15. Roderigo, in *Othello.*
16. Petruchio, in *The Taming of the Shrew.*
17. Iachimo, in *Cymbeline.*
18. Launce, in *The Two Gentlemen of Verona.*
19. Ajax, in *Troilus and Cressida.*
20. *Twelfth Night.*

4. "SUNDRY CONTEMPLATIONS"

1. Julius Caesar.
2. Antony's, in *Antony and Cleopatra.*
3. Benedick, in *Much Ado About Nothing.*
4. Puck, in *A Midsummer-Night's Dream.*
5. Gratiano, in *The Merchant of Venice.*
6. *Richard III.*
7. Mistress Page, in *The Merry Wives of Windsor.*
8. Antiochus, in *Pericles.*
9. Aaron, in *Titus Andronicus.*
10. They are dogs, in *The Taming of the Shrew.*
11. Romeo, in *Romeo and Juliet.*

12. Priam, in *Troilus and Cressida*.
13. *The Tempest*.
14. Biron, in *Love's Labour's Lost*.
15. Antigonus, in *The Winter's Tale*.
16. Clown Feste, in *Twelfth Night*.
17. Othello.
18. The Duke of York and his sons, in *Henry VI, Part III*.
19. Orlando, in *As You Like It*.
20. Italy, in *All's Well That Ends Well*.

5. "SUNDRY CONTEMPLATIONS"

1. Coriolanus.
2. Bolingbroke, in *Richard II*.
3. Lucius, in *Titus Andronicus*.
4. Vincentio, in *Measure for Measure*.
5. One of the entertainments on the list submitted to Theseus for his wedding, in *A Midsummer-Night's Dream*.
6. Cleopatra, in *Antony and Cleopatra*.
7. Celia says to Rosalind: "You must borrow me Gargantua's mouth," in *As You Like It*.
8. *The Comedy of Errors*.
9. "Husbandry," in *Hamlet*.
10. "Consumption of the purse," in *Henry IV, Part II*.
11. Biron, in *Love's Labour's Lost*.
12. Romeo, in *Romeo and Juliet*.
13. Joan of Arc's, in *Henry VI, Part I*.
14. "The Law Salique," in *Henry V*.
15. Cardinal Wolsey, in *Henry VIII*.
16. Othello.
17. "Opinion," in *Pericles*.
18. Countess of Rousillon, in *All's Well That Ends Well*.

19. The servants of the Montagues and Capulets, in *Romeo and Juliet*.
20. A page turned down in "The Tale of Tereus" is discovered by Iachimo in Imogen's boudoir, in *Cymbeline*.

6. "SUNDRY CONTEMPLATIONS"

1. The Bastard, in *King John*.
2. Mark Antony, in *Julius Caesar*.
3. Menenius Agrippa, in *Coriolanus*.
4. Richard II.
5. Belarius, in *Cymbeline*.
6. "Thou shalt not steal," in *Measure for Measure*.
7. The Ghost, in *Hamlet*.
8. Macmorris, in *Henry V*.
9. Othello's, in *Othello*.
10. Duke of Suffolk, in *Henry VI, Part II*.
11. The marriage by proxy of Henry VI to Margaret of Anjou, in *Henry VI, Part II*.
12. Cleopatra, in *Antony and Cleopatra*.
13. Cardinal Wolsey's, in *Henry VIII*.
14. Pompey, in *Measure for Measure*.
15. Bassanio, in *The Merchant of Venice*.
16. Petruchio, in *The Taming of the Shrew*.
17. Gonzalo, in *The Tempest*.
18. Apemantus, in *Timon of Athens*.
19. Nestor, in *Troilus and Cressida*.
20. Duke Senior and his "many merry men," in *As You Like It*.

7. "SUNDRY CONTEMPLATIONS"

1. Julia, in *The Two Gentlemen of Verona*.
2. The Oracle of Delphos', in *The Winter's Tale*.

3. Cardinal Wolsey, in *Henry VIII.*
4. Lavinia, in *Titus Andronicus.*
5. Henry VIII and Claudius in *Hamlet.*
6. Duke of Gloucester, in *Richard III.*
7. Queen Margaret, in the three parts of *Henry VI* and *Richard III.*
8. Malvolio, in *Twelfth Night.*
9. A play that Hamlet considers excellent, containing an account of the murder of Priam, in *Hamlet.*
10. Beatrice and Benedick, in *Much Ado About Nothing.*
11. Brabantio, in *Othello.*
12. Oberon and Titania, in *A Midsummer-Night's Dream.*
13. Antiochus, in *Pericles.*
14. Slender, in *The Merry Wives of Windsor.*
15. Antonio's, in *The Merchant of Venice.*
16. They are all prisoners, in *Measure for Measure.*
17. Macbeth.
18. The moon which is never more than a month old, in *Love's Labour's Lost.*
19. Goneril and Regan, in *King Lear.*
20. The volunteers King John leads to France, in *King John.*

8. "SUNDRY CONTEMPLATIONS"

1. Bertram, in *All's Well That Ends Well.*
2. Sir Hugh Evans, in *The Merry Wives of Windsor.*
3. *Love's Labour's Lost.*
4. Scarus', in *Antony and Cleopatra.*
5. Queen to *Cymbeline.*
6. Celia and Rosalind, in *As You Like It.*
7. King Hamlet's, in *Hamlet.*
8. Edmund Mortimer, in *Henry IV, Part I.*

9. In the Temple-garden at London where the white rose was chosen for York and the red rose for Lancaster, in *Henry VI, Part I.*

10. Lady Grey who marries Edward IV, in *Henry VI, Part III.*

11. Cassius, in *Julius Caesar.*

12. Jack Cade, in *Henry VI, Part II.*

13. Edgar, in *King Lear.*

14. Shylock, in *The Merchant of Venice.*

15. "Low," in *Much Ado About Nothing.*

16. Theseus, in *A Midsummer-Night's Dream.*

17. The handkerchief that Othello gave Desdemona, in *Othello.*

18. They are the six gates of Troy, in *Troilus and Cressida.*

19. Duke of Bedford, in *Henry VI, Part I.*

20. *Pericles.*

9. "SUNDRY CONTEMPLATIONS"

1. The two Antipholuses and the two Dromios, in *The Comedy of Errors.*

2. First Witch, in *Macbeth.*

3. Bertram, in *All's Well That Ends Well.*

4. Henry V.

5. Cassius, in *Julius Caesar.*

6. One year. See *Henry IV, Part I*, Act 1, Scene 1.

7. *Julius Caesar.*

8. Elinor, in *King John.*

9. Earl of Gloucester, in *King Lear.*

10. "Salmons," in *Henry V.*

11. Claudio, in *Measure for Measure.*

12. Beatrice, in *Much Ado About Nothing.*

13. Lysander, in *A Midsummer-Night's Dream.*
14. Anne Page, in *The Merry Wives of Windsor.*
15. Bassanio, in *The Merchant of Venice.*
16. Adam, in *As You Like It.*
17. Junius Brutus, in *Coriolanus.*
18. "Rumour," in *Henry IV, Part II.*
19. Costard, in *Love's Labour's Lost.*
20. Marcellus, in *Hamlet.*

10. "SUNDRY CONTEMPLATIONS"

1. Baptista, in *The Taming of the Shrew.*
2. Costard, in *Love's Labour's Lost.*
3. Queen Elizabeth, in *Richard III.*
4. John of Gaunt, in *Richard II.*
5. Ireland, in *Macbeth* and *Henry VI, Part II.*
6. Iago, in *Othello.*
7. Julius Caesar.
8. Coriolanus.
9. The asp, in *Antony and Cleopatra.*
10. Autolycus, in *The Winter's Tale.*
11. *Twelfth Night.*
12. Parolles, in *All's Well That Ends Well.*
13. Hector, in *Troilus and Cressida.*
14. Aaron, in *Titus Andronicus.*
15. Saturninus and Tamora, in *Titus Andronicus.*
16. Timon of Athens.
17. Miranda, in *The Tempest.*
18. *Romeo and Juliet.*
19. Hamlet.
20. Thaliard, in *Pericles.*

11. "SUNDRY CONTEMPLATIONS"

1. Anne Bullen, in *Henry VIII*.
2. Earl of Warwick, in *Henry VI, Part III*.
3. Cassius, in *Julius Caesar*.
4. Ariel, in *The Tempest*.
5. King Henry, in *Henry VI, Part I*.
6. He was killed while hunting the lion, in *Henry V*.
7. Sometime between the first and second parts of *Henry IV*. She is "an honest man's wife" in *Part I*.
8. King Henry envies the Earl of Northumberland, in *Henry IV, Part I*.
9. Hamlet.
10. Rome, in *Cymbeline*.
11. Titus Lartius, in *Coriolanus*.
12. Adriana and Luciana, in *The Comedy of Errors*.
13. Chatillon, in *King John*.
14. Antony, in *Antony and Cleopatra*.
15. Edmund, in *King Lear*.
16. Frederick, in *As You Like It*.
17. The Witches, in *Macbeth*.
18. Countess of Rousillon, in *All's Well That Ends Well*.
19. Isabella, in *Measure for Measure*.
20. *Love's Labour's Lost*.

12. "SUNDRY CONTEMPLATIONS"

1. The Marquis is Edward's stepson, in *Richard III*.
2. Katharina and Bianca, in *The Taming of the Shrew*.

3. *A Midsummer-Night's Dream.*
4. The Poet, in *Timon of Athens.*
5. Saturninus and Bassianus, in *Titus Andronicus.*
6. Paris, in *Troilus and Cressida.*
7. *The Merry Wives of Windsor.*
8. Bassanio, in *The Merchant of Venice.*
9. "That he should weep for her," in *Hamlet.*
10. Tarsus, in *Pericles.*
11. Iago says it to Roderigo, in *Othello.*
12. Richard II.
13. Launce, in *The Two Gentlemen of Verona.*
14. Leontes, in *The Winter's Tale.*
15. Parolles, in *All's Well That Ends Well.*
16. Cleopatra, in *Antony and Cleopatra.*
17. Richard is referring to Lady Anne, in *Richard III.*
18. *Romeo and Juliet.*
19. Prospero, in *The Tempest.*
20. Christopher Sly, in *The Taming of the Shrew.*

13. "SUNDRY CONTEMPLATIONS"

1. Adam, in *As You Like It.*
2. The Dauphin loses to Joan of Arc, in *Henry VI, Part I.*
3. Duchess of Gloucester, in *Henry VI, Part II.*
4. "Duke of Buckingham."
5. Mark Antony, in *Julius Caesar.*
6. Mariana, in *Measure for Measure.*
7. Grumio strikes Curtis, in *The Taming of the Shrew.*
8. Queen Elinor, in *King John.*
9. First Witch, in *Macbeth.*
10. "The pot" in a song, in *Love's Labour's Lost.*
11. On the platform before the castle, in *Hamlet.*

12. Desdemona, in *Othello*.
13. Iachimo, in *Cymbeline*.
14. Antipholus of Syracuse, in *The Comedy of Errors*.
15. Simple, in *The Merry Wives of Windsor*.
16. Coriolanus.
17. Lord Clifford, in *Henry VI, Part III*.
18. *Hamlet*.
19. "Speak of me as I am," in *Othello*.
20. Falstaff, when Prince Henry says, "I could have better spared a better man," in *Henry IV, Part I*.

14. "SUNDRY CONTEMPLATIONS"

1. Timon of Athens.
2. Portia's, in *The Merchant of Venice*.
3. Thaisa, in *Pericles*.
4. Tamora, in *Titus Andronicus*.
5. Miranda, in *The Tempest*.
6. Hermione, in *The Winter's Tale*.
7. Ajax, in *Troilus and Cressida*.
8. Bertram, in *All's Well That Ends Well*.
9. The stab of Brutus on Caesar, in *Julius Caesar*.
10. Bardolph.
11. Christopher Sly, in *The Taming of the Shrew*.
12. Edmund, Earl of Rutland, in *Henry VI, Part III*.
13. Oberon and Titania (the betrothed pair are Hippolyta and Theseus), in *A Midsummer-Night's Dream*.
14. Duke of Clarence, in *Richard III*.
15. Sir John Falstaff, in *The Merry Wives of Windsor*.
16. Queen Mab's, in *Romeo and Juliet*.
17. *Macbeth*.
18. Valentine, in *The Two Gentlemen of Verona*.

19. "Imagination," in *A Midsummer-Night's Dream*.
20. Richard to John of Gaunt, in *Richard II*.

15. "SUNDRY CONTEMPLATIONS"

1. Shylock, in *The Merchant of Venice*.
2. *Measure for Measure*.
3. Edmund, in *King Lear*.
4. Duncan to Lady Macbeth, in *Macbeth*.
5. Antipholus of Syracuse, in *The Comedy of Errors*.
6. "Ambition," in *Henry VIII*.
7. Sir Nathaniel, in *Love's Labour's Lost*.
8. King Lewis XI (about Edward IV), in *Henry VI, Part III*.
9. Philip Faulconbridge, in *King John*.
10. Edward IV, Edward V, and Richard III.
11. "Slander," in *Cymbeline*.
12. Sir John Falstaff, in *Henry IV, Part II*.
13. "The Murder of Gonzago," in *Hamlet*.
14. Fluellen, in *Henry V*.
15. Coriolanus.
16. Hotspur, in *Henry IV, Part I*.
17. Celia, in *As You Like It*.
18. Cleopatra, in *Antony and Cleopatra*.
19. Lord Talbot, in *Henry VI, Part I*.
20. Cassius, in *Julius Caesar*.

16. "SUNDRY CONTEMPLATIONS"

1. Euriphile (deceased wife to Belarius), in *Cymbeline*.
2. "In battalions," in *Hamlet*.

3. Volumnia, in *Coriolanus*.
4. Queen Mab, in *Romeo and Juliet*.
5. "Second Murderer" of Duke of Clarence, in *Richard III*.
6. Owen Glendower, in *Henry IV, Part I*.
7. Benedick, in *Much Ado About Nothing*.
8. Brabantio, in *Othello*.
9. Egeus, in *A Midsummer-Night's Dream*.
10. Sir Hugh Evans, in *The Merry Wives of Windsor*.
11. Shylock, in *The Merchant of Venice*.
12. Claudio, in *Measure for Measure*.
13. Lady Macbeth and *Macbeth*.
14. Don Adriano de Armado, in *Love's Labour's Lost*.
15. Cordelia's, in *King Lear*.
16. Earl of Salisbury's, in *King John*.
17. "Lowliness," in *Julius Caesar*.
18. Cardinal Wolsey, in *Henry VIII*.
19. Doll Tearsheet, in *Henry IV, Part II*.
20. Richard II.

17. "SUNDRY CONTEMPLATIONS"

1. Antipholus of Syracuse, in *The Comedy of Errors*.
2. Mistress Quickly's, in *The Merry Wives of Windsor*.
3. Romeo's, in *Romeo and Juliet*.
4. Chiron and Demetrius fight over Lavinia, in *Titus Andronicus*.
5. Antigonus, in *The Winter's Tale*.
6. The Witches, in *Macbeth*.
7. Hamlet, Rosencrantz, and Guildenstern are having a discussion as to whether the world is a prison or not, in *Hamlet*.

8. The proud man's "glassy essence," in *Measure for Measure*.
9. Orlando, in *As You Like It*.
10. Miranda, in *The Tempest*.
11. Hotspur, in *Henry IV, Part I*.
12. Owen Glendower.
13. Achilles and Patroclus, in *Troilus and Cressida*.
14. Duke of Clarence, in *Richard III*.
15. Coriolanus's, in *Coriolanus*.
16. Richard II.
17. Antiochus and his daughter, in *Pericles*.
18. Cassio, in *Othello*.
19. Theseus, in *A Midsummer-Night's Dream*.
20. Don Pedro, in *Much Ado About Nothing*.

18. "SUNDRY CONTEMPLATIONS"

1. Lady Macbeth, in *Macbeth*.
2. Adriana, in *The Comedy of Errors*.
3. Pompey, in *Antony and Cleopatra*.
4. Dogberry, in *Much Ado About Nothing*.
5. Sir John Falstaff, in *Henry IV, Parts I and II*, and *The Merry Wives of Windsor*.
6. Ajax, in *Troilus and Cressida*.
7. Othello.
8. Queen Anne, in *Richard III*.
9. Jessica, in *The Merchant of Venice*.
10. Timon of Athens.
11. "Concealment" of her love, in *Twelfth Night*.
12. Pythagoras in *Twelfth Night, The Merchant of Venice*, and *As You Like It*.
13. Katharina's, in *The Taming of the Shrew*.
14. The Old Shepherd who discovers gold wrapped in a

bearing-cloth when he rescues Perdita, in *The Winter's Tale*.

15. King Hamlet, in *Hamlet*.
16. Edmund Mortimer, in *Henry IV, Part I*.
17. Rouen, in *Henry VI, Part I*.
18. A fool Jaques met in the forest, in *As You Like It*.
19. Cranmer, Archbishop of Canterbury, in *Henry VIII*.
20. Duke of Gloucester, in *Richard III*.

19. "SUNDRY CONTEMPLATIONS"

1. Duchess of Gloucester, in *Henry VI, Part II*.
2. John Hume.
3. "Authority," in *The Winter's Tale*.
4. Hamlet.
5. Nym, Bardolph and Pistol, in *Henry V*.
6. Brutus's in *Julius Caesar*.
7. King John.
8. Armado uses this in a letter, in *Love's Labour's Lost*.
9. Owen Glendower's, in *Henry IV, Part I*.
10. Young Marcius, in *Coriolanus*.
11. Richard Plantagenet and the Earl of Somerset, in *Henry VI, Part I*.
12. "Sleep," in *Macbeth*.
13. Imogen's, in *Cymbeline*.
14. Lavache, in *All's Well That Ends Well*.
15. King Ferdinand, in *Love's Labour's Lost*.
16. Eros (Antony is the friend), in *Antony and Cleopatra*.
17. *The Merchant of Venice*.
18. Mariana, in *Measure for Measure*.
19. Rosalind, in *As You Like It*.
20. King Lear.

20. "SUNDRY CONTEMPLATIONS"

1. Imogen, in *Cymbeline*.
2. Bassianus's, in *Titus Andronicus*.
3. Doctor Caius and Sir Hugh Evans, in *The Merry Wives of Windsor*.
4. Macbeth.
5. Brutus, in *Julius Caesar*.
6. Robert Faulconbridge, the elder, in *King John*.
7. Earl of Warwick, in *Henry VI, Part III*.
8. Launcelot Gobbo's sand-blind father does not recognize him, in *The Merchant of Venice*.
9. Princess Katharine and Alice, in *Henry V*, and Dr. Caius, in *The Merry Wives of Windsor*.
10. Cassandra, in *Troilus and Cressida*.
11. *The Taming of the Shrew*.
12. Richard III.
13. Marina, in *Pericles*.
14. King Lear.
15. Goneril.
16. "Purple," in *A Midsummer-Night's Dream*.
17. Antonio, in *The Tempest*.
18. Holofernes, in *Love's Labour's Lost*.
19. Nym's, in *Henry V* and *The Merry Wives of Windsor*.
20. Othello.

21. "SUNDRY CONTEMPLATIONS"

1. Henry VI, in *Henry VI, Part III*.
2. King Richard's, in *Richard III*.

3. Pinch, in *The Comedy of Errors.*
4. Yorick, in *Hamlet.*
5. Orlando, in *As You Like It.*
6. Biron, in *Love's Labour's Lost.*
7. Duncan's, after his murder, in *Macbeth.*
8. Joan.
9. Jessica, in *The Merchant of Venice.*
10. Oberon, in *A Midsummer-Night's Dream.*
11. Cardinal Wolsey, in *Henry VIII.*
12. Othello.
13. Aaron, in *Titus Andronicus.*
14. Thaisa, in *Pericles.*
15. Tranio, in *The Taming of the Shrew.*
16. Julius Caesar.
17. Artemidorus.
18. "Peace," in *Coriolanus.*
19. Mercutio is speaking of Tybalt, in *Romeo and Juliet.*
20. His "brag."

22. "SUNDRY CONTEMPLATIONS

1. "Love," in *As You Like It.*
2. Hotspur, in *Henry IV, Part I.*
3. Ophelia, in *Hamlet.*
4. Earl of Gloucester, in *King Lear.*
5. Duncan, in *Macbeth.*
6. Edward and Richard, in *Richard III.*
7. King Edward IV and Queen Elizabeth.
8. "That, that is, is," in *Twelfth Night.*
9. Dogberry, in *Much Ado About Nothing.*
10. It means an animal, in *A Midsummer-Night's Dream.*
11. Falstaff, in *The Merry Wives of Windsor.*

12. Bassanio, who is heavily in debt, in *The Merchant of Venice.*
13. "The cuckoo" in a song, in *Love's Labour's Lost.*
14. King John.
15. Hubert de Burgh.
16. Portia, in *Julius Caesar.*
17. "Misery," in *The Tempest.*
18. Cloten and Imogen, in *Cymbeline.*
19. Macbeth.
20. Juliet, in *Romeo and Juliet.*

23. "SUNDRY CONTEMPLATIONS"

1. Mercutio, in *Romeo and Juliet.*
2. King Lear.
3. Queen, in *Richard II.*
4. Duke of Gloucester, in *Henry VI, Part III.*
5. Claudius, in *Hamlet.*
6. Celia and Oliver, in *As You Like It.*
7. Verges, in *Much Ado About Nothing.*
8. Henry V.
9. "Trash," in *Othello.*
10. Antonio's, in *The Merchant of Venice.*
11. The basket of laundry, in *The Merry Wives of Windsor.*
12. Guiderius, in *Cymbeline.*
13. Two: Sir Hugh Evans, in *The Merry Wives of Windsor;* and Fluellen, in *Henry V.*
14. Duke of Gloucester, in *Henry VI, Part III.*
15. Duchess of Gloucester, in *Henry VI, Part II.*
16. Julius Caesar's, in *Julius Caesar.*
17. Falstaff, in *Henry IV, Part I.*
18. Queen Anne, in *Henry VIII.*

19. King John.
20. Puck, in *A Midsummer-Night's Dream.*

24. "SUNDRY CONTEMPLATIONS"

1. Mercutio, in *Romeo and Juliet.*
2. Edgar, in *King Lear.*
3. Helen, in *Troilus and Cressida.*
4. "Revenges," in *Twelfth Night.*
5. Silvia, in *The Two Gentlemen of Verona.*
6. King Ferdinand and his lords, in *Love's Labour's Lost.*
7. Hermione, in *The Winter's Tale.*
8. Banquo's, in *Macbeth.*
9. To help Bassanio select the right casket, in *The Merchant of Venice.*
10. Gonzalo, in *The Tempest.*
11. Prince Arthur, in *King John.*
12. Marcus Antonius and Marcus Brutus, in *Julius Caesar.*
13. Cardinal Wolsey, in *Henry VIII.*
14. Queen Margaret, in *Henry VI, Part III.*
15. (a) Pistol, (b) Slender, in *The Merry Wives of Windsor.*
16. Richard III.
17. Imogen, in *Cymbeline.*
18. Polonius, who says it, is a very talkative old man, in *Hamlet.*
19. Touchstone, in *As You Like It.*
20. Daughter of Antiochus, in *Pericles.*

25. "SUNDRY CONTEMPLATIONS"

1. Katharina, in *The Taming of the Shrew.*
2. *The Tempest.*

3. The Old Athenian, in *Timon of Athens.*
4. Menelaus, in *Troilus and Cressida.*
5. Henry V.
6. Autolycus, in *The Winter's Tale.*
7. Iras, in *Antony and Cleopatra.*
8. Portia, in *The Merchant of Venice.*
9. Lady Macbeth's "little hand," in *Macbeth.*
10. Duke Vincentio, in *Measure for Measure.*
11. Lady Capulet, in *Romeo and Juliet.*
12. Helena and Hermia, in *A Midsummer-Night's Dream.*
13. Leonato, in *Much Ado About Nothing.*
14. *Othello.*
15. Othello kills Desdemona, and Iago kills Emilia, in *Othello.*
16. Richard III.
17. Claudius's, in *Hamlet.*
18. Richard II.
19. King Lear.
20. Capulet's, in *Romeo and Juliet.*

26. "SUNDRY CONTEMPLATIONS"

1. Romeo, in *Romeo and Juliet.*
2. In the letter Maria writes to Malvolio, in *Twelfth Night.*
3. *Richard III.*
4. Margaret, Elizabeth and Anne.
5. Roderigo, in *Othello.*
6. Bottom, in *A Midsummer-Night's Dream.*
7. Dionyza, in *Pericles.*
8. Sir John Falstaff, in *The Merry Wives of Windsor.*
9. In the golden casket, in *The Merchant of Venice.*
10. Antony, in *Antony and Cleopatra.*
11. Earl of Kent, in *King Lear.*

12. The Bastard, in *King John*.
13. Portia, in *Julius Caesar*.
14. Edward IV, in *Henry VI, Part III*.
15. Hamlet calls Polonius one, in *Hamlet*.
16. Pinch, in *The Comedy of Errors*.
17. Saturninus, in *Titus Andronicus*.
18. Orlando, in *As You Like It*.
19. Galen, in *The Merry Wives of Windsor*, *All's Well That Ends Well*, *Coriolanus*, and *Henry IV, Part II*.
20. Perdita, in *The Winter's Tale*.

27. "SUNDRY CONTEMPLATIONS"

1. Mercutio, in *Romeo and Juliet*.
2. Queen Margaret, in *Richard III*.
3. Ajax, in *Troilus and Cressida*.
4. Pericles.
5. "That sweet sleep Which thou owedst yesterday," in *Othello*.
6. Cupid's, in *Love's Labour's Lost*.
7. The news that Antonio is bankrupt, in *The Merchant of Venice*.
8. Gonzalo, in *The Tempest*.
9. Falstaff, in *The Merry Wives of Windsor*.
10. After the assassination, in *Julius Caesar*.
11. Prince Arthur, in *King John*.
12. Helena, in *All's Well That Ends Well*.
13. Earl of Suffolk, in *Henry VI, Part I*.
14. Margaret.
15. Coriolanus.
16. The uncle of Cymbeline who, in the time of Julius Caesar, granted a tribute to Rome.

17. Mistress Quickly and Doll Tearsheet, in *Henry IV, Part II.*
18. "Pyramus and Thisbe," in *A Midsummer-Night's Dream.*
19. Laertes, in *Hamlet.*
20. Sir Andrew Aguecheek, in *Twelfth Night.*

28. "SUNDRY CONTEMPLATIONS"

1. King Lear.
2. Lady Macbeth, in *Macbeth.*
3. Slender, in *The Merry Wives of Windsor.*
4. "Northumberland," in several plays.
5. Othello, "Like the base Indian," in *Othello.*
6. Mytilene, in *Pericles.*
7. Juliet, in *Romeo and Juliet.*
8. Richard II.
9. Alonso's, in *The Tempest.*
10. Christopher Sly, in *The Taming of the Shrew.*
11. Timon of Athens.
12. Duke of Gloucester, in *Richard III.*
13. Tamora, in *Titus Andronicus.*
14. Menenius Agrippa, in *Coriolanus.*
15. Calchas, in *Troilus and Cressida.*
16. Rosalind and Celia, in *As You Like It.*
17. Sebastian, in *Twelfth Night.*
18. Antonio.
19. Duke of Milan, in *The Two Gentlemen of Verona.*
20. Bertram, in *All's Well That Ends Well.*

29. "SUNDRY CONTEMPLATIONS"

1. Lady Mortimer, in *Henry IV, Part I.*
2. Flavius and Marullus, in *Julius Caesar.*

3. Cloten's, in *Cymbeline*.
4. Sir John Falstaff, in *Henry V*.
5. That Coriolanus will not attack Rome, in *Coriolanus*.
6. Parolles, in *All's Well That Ends Well*.
7. "Good name," in *Othello*.
8. Mistress Quickly, in *The Merry Wives of Windsor*.
9. Duchess of Gloucester, in *Henry VI, Part II*.
10. "Thy habit" or "apparel," in *Hamlet*.
11. King Henry, in *Henry VI, Part III*.
12. Earl of Warwick and Duke of Clarence.
13. At Ninus's tomb, in *A Midsummer-Night's Dream*.
14. Edgar, in *King Lear*.
15. The Italian girl that Bertram pretends to love, in *All's Well That Ends Well*.
16. Henry Percy and Bolingbroke, in *Richard II* and *Henry IV, Part I*.
17. Orlando, in *As You Like It*.
18. "Beggars," in *Romeo and Juliet*.
19. Baptista, in *The Taming of the Shrew*.
20. In the silver casket, in *The Merchant of Venice*.

30. "SUNDRY CONTEMPLATIONS"

1. Lord Talbot, in *Henry VI, Part I*.
2. Ariel, in *The Tempest*.
3. Baptista, Katharina and Bianca, in *The Taming of the Shrew*.
4. Mercutio, in *Romeo and Juliet*.
5. Bishop of Ely, in *Richard III*.
6. Lord Say is ordered beheaded by Jack Cade, in *Henry VI, Part II*.
7. Simonides, in *Pericles*.
8. King of Norway, in *Macbeth*.

9. Iago, in *Othello.*
10. William Page, in *The Merry Wives of Windsor.*
11. "Mercy," in *The Merchant of Venice.*
12. *Henry V.*
13. Biron, in *Love's Labour's Lost.*
14. Mark Antony, in *Julius Caesar.*
15. "Reputation," in *As You Like It.*
16. Polonius's, in *Hamlet.*
17. Lady Northumberland, in *Henry IV, Part II.*
18. Sir John Falstaff, in *Henry IV, Part I, Henry IV, Part II,* and *The Merry Wives of Windsor.*
19. Tamora, in *Titus Andronicus.*
20. Richard, in *Henry VI, Part III.*

31. "SUNDRY CONTEMPLATIONS"

1. King Henry, in *Henry VI, Part II.*
2. Lodovico, in *Othello.*
3. Portia, in *Julius Caesar.*
4. Duke of Buckingham, in *Richard III.*
5. Romeo's in *Romeo and Juliet.*
6. Padua, in *The Taming of the Shrew.*
7. Pistol, in *Henry IV, Part II.*
8. It means mischief, according to Hamlet.
9. Posthumus, in *Cymbeline.*
10. Volumnia, in *Coriolanus.*
11. *The Comedy of Errors.*
12. Touchstone's, in *As You Like It.*
13. *Antony and Cleopatra.*
14. "In ourselves," in *Julius Caesar.*
15. "Thy father," meaning Alonso, in *The Tempest.*
16. Holofernes, in *Love's Labour's Lost.*

17. "Treasons, stratagems and spoils," in *The Merchant of Venice*.
18. Peter Quince, in *A Midsummer-Night's Dream*.
19. Duke of York, in *Richard II*.
20. Bolingbroke.

32. "SUNDRY CONTEMPLATIONS"

1. *The Merry Wives of Windsor*.
2. Lewis the Dauphin, in *Henry V*.
3. Duncan, in *Macbeth*.
4. Cranmer, in *Henry VIII*.
5. Iago's, in *Othello*.
6. Macbeth.
7. Banquo's ghost.
8. Julia, in *The Two Gentlemen of Verona*.
9. Sir Toby Belch, in *Twelfth Night*.
10. Troilus and Paris, in *Troilus and Cressida*.
11. On the island, in *The Tempest*.
12. Phrynia and Timandra, in *Timon of Athens*.
13. Hortensio, in *The Taming of the Shrew*.
14. "Parting," in *Romeo and Juliet*.
15. Richard III.
16. Richard's, in *Richard II*.
17. The House of Lancaster.
18. Julius Caesar.
19. The Turkish Fleet, in *Othello*.
20. Antonio, in *The Merchant of Venice*.

33. "SUNDRY CONTEMPLATIONS"

1. Bolingbroke's, in *Richard II*.
2. Richard II.

3. Pericles.
4. Borachio, in *Much Ado About Nothing*.
5. The marriage of Claudio and Hero.
6. The wedding of Hippolyta and Theseus, in *A Midsummer-Night's Dream*.
7. Claudio, in *Measure for Measure*.
8. Duncan's deceased Queen, in *Macbeth*.
9. The birthday of Cassius, in *Julius Caesar*.
10. Portia, in *The Merchant of Venice*.
11. *Henry VI, Part II*.
12. King Ferdinand and his followers, in *Love's Labour's Lost*.
13. King Henry, in *Henry IV, Part II*.
14. Agincourt, in *Henry V*.
15. Guiderius and Arviragus, in *Cymbeline*.
16. Polonius, in *Hamlet*.
17. Goneril, in *King Lear*.
18. *As You Like It*.
19. Bertram is glad to hear his wife is dead, in *All's Well That Ends Well*.
20. Katharina, in *The Taming of the Shrew*.

34. "SUNDRY CONTEMPLATIONS"

1. Othello.
2. Macduff, in *Macbeth*.
3. The Nurse, in *Romeo and Juliet*.
4. Antony, Octavius and Lepidus, in *Julius Caesar*.
5. Queen Margaret, in *Henry VI, Part III*.
6. Princess of France, in *Love's Labour's Lost*.
7. The Ghost of King Hamlet, the second time he appears to Hamlet.

8. Gertrude's, in *Hamlet*.
9. Orlando, in *As You Like It*.
10. Two: Isabel, in *Henry V;* and Cordelia, in *King Lear*.
11. Cordelia's in *King Lear*.
12. Queen of Britain, in *Cymbeline*.
13. Thaisa and Pericles, in *Pericles*.
14. Othello.
15. Demetrius, in *Titus Andronicus*.
16. Lavinia.
17. Tranio (disguised as Lucentio), in *The Taming of the Shrew*.
18. Caliban, in *The Tempest*.
19. *Macbeth*.
20. Pistol, in *Henry IV, Part II, Henry V*, and *The Merry Wives of Windsor*.

35. "SUNDRY CONTEMPLATIONS"

1. Henry IV, in *Henry IV, Part II*.
2. Oliver (about Orlando), in *As You Like It*.
3. This is part of the gibberish used to trap Parolles, in *All's Well That Ends Well*.
4. Timon of Athens.
5. Saturninus, in *Titus Andronicus*.
6. Keeping wassail, in *Hamlet*.
7. Shylock, in *The Merchant of Venice*.
8. Jessica, in *The Merchant of Venice*.
9. Othello.
10. None.
11. Hermione's, in *The Winter's Tale*.
12. Titus Andronicus.
13. Miranda, in *The Tempest*.

14. Shrewsbury, in *Henry IV, Part I.*
15. Elinor, in *King John;* and Elizabeth and Margaret, in *Richard III.*
16. Hermia, in *A Midsummer-Night's Dream.*
17. Petruchio, in *The Taming of the Shrew.*
18. Malcolm, speaking of Macbeth.
19. Marcus Brutus, in *Julius Caesar.*
20. Duke of Gloucester and Bishop of Winchester, in *Henry VI, Part I.*

36. "SUNDRY CONTEMPLATIONS"

1. *The Winter's Tale.*
2. Cassio, in *Othello.*
3. Polonius, in *Hamlet.*
4. Desdemona, in *Othello.*
5. One—Jamy, in *Henry V.*
6. Antipholus of Ephesus, in *The Comedy of Errors.*
7. Valeria, in *Coriolanus.*
8. Rosencrantz and Guildenstern die in place of Hamlet.
9. Philarmonus, a soothsayer, in *Cymbeline.*
10. Cleopatra, in *Antony and Cleopatra.*
11. Caesarion, the son of Cleopatra and (supposedly) Julius Caesar.
12. Jack Cade, in *Henry VI, Part II.*
13. Lady Macduff, in *Macbeth.*
14. Petruchio, in *The Taming of the Shrew.*
15. Titus Andronicus.
16. Prospero has Ariel, in *The Tempest.*
17. In a poem Orlando writes to Rosalind, in *As You Like It.*
18. The three musicians who are hired to furnish music for Juliet's wedding, in *Romeo and Juliet.*

19. Pandarus, in *Troilus and Cressida*.
20. The Duke is their father-in-law, in *Henry VIII*.

37. "SUNDRY CONTEMPLATIONS"

1. Petruchio, in *The Taming of the Shrew*.
2. *Richard III*.
3. Pericles.
4. "Confirmations strong As proofs of holy writ," in *Othello*.
5. *The Merchant of Venice*.
6. A bear, mentioned in *The Merry Wives of Windsor*.
7. The Fool, in *King Lear*.
8. Cassius, in *Julius Caesar*.
9. Queen Katharine and Henry VIII.
10. Lord Clifford, in *Henry VI, Part III*.
11. Lord Mowbray, in *Henry IV, Part II*.
12. Hamlet.
13. Phebe has learned that Rosalind is a girl, in *As You Like It*.
14. Lady Macbeth, in *Macbeth*.
15. Fortinbras, in *Hamlet*.
16. Volumnia, in *Coriolanus*.
17. "The fashion," in *Much Ado About Nothing*.
18. Lady Montague, in *Romeo and Juliet*.
19. Proculeius, in *Antony and Cleopatra*.
20. Orlando, in *As You Like It*.

38. "SUNDRY CONTEMPLATIONS"

1. "The toothache," in *Much Ado About Nothing*.
2. Marcus Brutus, in *Julius Caesar*.
3. Sir Nathaniel and Holofernes, in *Love's Labour's Lost*.

4. Vincentio says it to Isabella, in *Measure for Measure*.
5. Banquo, in *Macbeth*.
6. Host of the Garter Inn, in *The Merry Wives of Windsor*.
7. Goneril and Regan, in *King Lear*.
8. Claudio, in *Much Ado About Nothing*.
9. Desdemona, in *Othello*.
10. Ghost of Lady Anne, in *Richard III*.
11. Marina, in *Pericles*.
12. Baptista, in *The Taming of the Shrew*.
13. Miranda and Ferdinand, in *The Tempest*.
14. The Banditti, in *Timon of Athens*.
15. Little Lucius, in *Titus Andronicus*.
16. Cressida's, in *Troilus and Cressida*.
17. Malvolio, in *Twelfth Night*.
18. Ophelia, in *Hamlet*.
19. Julia is speaking to Proteus, in *The Two Gentlemen of Verona*.
20. *Henry V*.

39. "SUNDRY CONTEMPLATIONS"

1. Julius Caesar.
2. Octavius Caesar.
3. Feste the Clown, in *Twelfth Night*.
4. Enobarbus, in *Antony and Cleopatra*.
5. *As You Like It*.
6. Hamlet.
7. Hotspur, in *Henry IV, Part I*.
8. In the epilogue to *Henry IV, Part II*, the Dancer says she will kneel and "pray for the queen."
9. *Romeo and Juliet*.
10. Othello.

11. Macbeth.
12. The charges against Falstaff and his followers, in *The Merry Wives of Windsor.*
13. Richard II.
14. Romeo and Juliet are to be so honored by their respective fathers-in-law.
15. Priam. This is mentioned in *Titus Andronicus.*
16. Aaron, in *Titus Andronicus.*
17. Achilles, in *Troilus and Cressida.*
18. Hector.
19. Polixenes, in *The Winter's Tale.*
20. The Ghost, in *Hamlet.*

40. "SUNDRY CONTEMPLATIONS"

1. Cleopatra, in *Antony and Cleopatra.*
2. Cicero, in *Julius Caesar.*
3. Oswald, in *King Lear.*
4. Henry VIII to Cardinal Wolsey.
5. "The poet's pen," in *A Midsummer-Night's Dream.*
6. Adriana, in *The Comedy of Errors.*
7. The Nevils, in *Henry VI, Part II.*
8. Ford, in *The Merry Wives of Windsor.*
9. Pindarus, servant to Cassius, in *Julius Caesar.*
10. The flowers that Gertrude scatters on Ophelia's grave, in *Hamlet.*
11. Petruchio, in *The Taming of the Shrew.*
12. Polixenes, in *The Winter's Tale.*
13. Hector's, in *Troilus and Cressida.*
14. Aaron, in *Titus Andronicus.*
15. Falstaff, in *Henry V.*
16. King of France, in *All's Well That Ends Well.*

17. Diana's, in *All's Well That Ends Well*.
18. Volumnia, in *Coriolanus*.
19. "A grave-maker," in *Hamlet*.
20. King Lear is bemoaning the fact that Cordelia will never be alive again.

"OUR SPECIAL DRIFT"

41. "OUR JUST AND LINEAL ENTRANCE"

1. Princess of France, in *Love's Labour's Lost*.
2. Portia, in *The Merchant of Venice*.
3. Rosalind, in *As You Like It*.
4. Ophelia, in *Hamlet*.
5. Juliet, in *Romeo and Juliet*.
6. Helena, in *All's Well That Ends Well*.
7. Miranda, in *The Tempest*.
8. Cleopatra, in *Antony and Cleopatra*.
9. Lavinia, in *Titus Andronicus*.
10. Volumnia, in *Coriolanus*.
11. Beatrice, in *Much Ado About Nothing*.
12. Desdemona, in *Othello*.
13. Queen Katharine, in *Henry VIII*.
14. Adriana, in *The Comedy of Errors*.
15. Imogen, in *Cymbeline*.
16. Silvia, in *The Two Gentlemen of Verona*.
17. Hermia, in *A Midsummer-Night's Dream*.
18. Olivia, in *Twelfth Night*.
19. Katharina, in *The Taming of the Shrew*.
20. Cressida, in *Troilus and Cressida*.

42. "ADMIT HIM ENTRANCE"

1. Titus Andronicus.
2. King Lear.
3. Philip Faulconbridge (The Bastard), in *King John.*
4. Henry V.
5. Hotspur, in *Henry IV, Part I.*
6. Prospero, in *The Tempest.*
7. Caius Marcius, in *Coriolanus.*
8. Orlando, in *As You Like It.*
9. Valentine, in *The Two Gentlemen of Verona.*
10. Timon of Athens.
11. Othello.
12. Macbeth.
13. Vincentio, in *Measure for Measure.*
14. Lysander, in *A Midsummer-Night's Dream.*
15. Pericles.
16. Petruchio, in *The Taming of the Shrew.*
17. Troilus, in *Troilus and Cressida.*
18. Antony, in *Antony and Cleopatra.*
19. Romeo, in *Romeo and Juliet.*
20. Hamlet.

43. "BY ANY OTHER NAME"

1. *b.* Cadwal, in *Cymbeline.*
2. *p.* Morgan, in *Cymbeline.*
3. *a.* Aliena, in *As You Like It.*
4. *c.* Caius, in *King Lear.*

5. *t.* Poor Tom, in *King Lear.*
6. *g.* Doricles, in *The Winter's Tale.*
7. *q.* Polydore, in *Cymbeline.*
8. *k.* Harry le Roy, in *Henry V.*
9. *m.* Licio, in *The Taming of the Shrew.*
10. *h.* Fidele, in *Cymbeline.*
11. *l.* Sir John Mortimer, in *Henry VI, Part II.*
12. *s.* Sebastian, in *The Two Gentlemen of Verona.*
13. *d.* Cambio, in *The Taming of the Shrew.*
14. *o.* Master Brook, in *The Merry Wives of Windsor.*
15. *f.* Doctor Balthasar, in *The Merchant of Venice.*
16. *j.* Ganymede, in *As You Like It.*
17. *r.* Roderigo, in *Twelfth Night.*
18. *n.* Lucentio, in *The Taming of the Shrew.*
19. *i.* Friar Lodowick, in *Measure for Measure.*
20. *e.* Cesario, in *Twelfth Night.*

44. "BRIDES AND BRIDEGROOMS ALL" Number 1

1. *r.* Richard III.
2. *i.* Henry VIII.
3. *s.* Touchstone, in *As You Like It.*
4. *b.* Benedick, in *Much Ado About Nothing.*
5. *m.* Lucentio, in *The Taming of the Shrew.*
6. *k.* Lewis, in *King John.*
7. *o.* Oliver, in *As You Like It.*
8. *j.* King of France, in *King Lear.*
9. *e.* Edward IV, in *Henry VI, Part III.*
10. *d.* Demetrius, in *A Midsummer-Night's Dream.*
11. *t.* Vincentio, in *Measure for Measure.*
12. *l.* Lorenzo, in *The Merchant of Venice.*

13. *q.* Proteus, in *The Two Gentlemen of Verona.*
14. *c.* Claudio, in *Measure for Measure.*
15. *h.* Henry V.
16. *a.* Bassianus, in *Titus Andronicus.*
17. *n.* Lysimachus, in *Pericles.*
18. *f.* Ferdinand, in *The Tempest.*
19. *g.* Florizel, in *The Winter's Tale.*
20. *p.* Orsino, in *Twelfth Night.*

45. "BRIDES AND BRIDEGROOMS ALL" Number 2

1. *h.* Fenton, in *The Merry Wives of Windsor.*
2. *e.* Bertram, in *All's Well That Ends Well.*
3. *l.* Lysander, in *A Midsummer-Night's Dream.*
4. *g.* Claudio, in *Much Ado About Nothing.*
5. *s.* Theseus, in *A Midsummer-Night's Dream.*
6. *o.* Petruchio, in *The Taming of the Shrew.*
7. *b.* Antipholus of Syracuse, in *The Comedy of Errors.*
8. *j.* Henry VI, in *Henry VI, Part I.*
9. *a.* Angelo, in *Measure for Measure.*
10. *i.* Gratiano, in *The Merchant of Venice.*
11. *c.* Antony, in *Antony and Cleopatra.*
12. *q.* Sebastian, in *Twelfth Night.*
13. *f.* Camillo, in *The Winter's Tale.*
14. *r.* Silvius, in *As You Like It.*
15. *d.* Bassanio, in *The Merchant of Venice.*
16. *m.* Orlando, in *As You Like It.*
17. *t.* Valentine, in *The Two Gentlemen of Verona.*
18. *p.* Saturninus, in *Titus Andronicus.*
19. *n.* Pericles.
20. *k.* Sir Toby Belch, in *Twelfth Night.*

46. "ALONE I DID IT"

1. Joan la Pucelle, in *Henry VI, Part I*.
2. Helena, in *All's Well That Ends Well*.
3. Troilus, in *Troilus and Cressida*.
4. Coriolanus.
5. Falstaff, in *Henry IV, Part I*.
6. Hamlet.
7. Juliet, in *Romeo and Juliet*.
8. Posthumus, in *Cymbeline*.
9. Flavius, in *Timon of Athens*.
10. Iago, in *Othello*.
11. Valentine, in *The Two Gentlemen of Verona*.
12. Antipholus of Syracuse, in *The Comedy of Errors*.
20. Macbeth.

47. "THE BITTER BREAD OF BANISHMENT"

1. The Duke Senior, in *As You Like It*.
2. Alcibiades, in *Timon of Athens*.
3. Duke of Suffolk, in *Henry VI, Part II*.

13. Sebastian, in *Twelfth Night*.
14. Angelo, in *Measure for Measure*.
15. Earl of Warwick, in *Henry VI, Part III*.
16. Aaron, in *Titus Andronicus*.
17. Biron, in *Love's Labour's Lost*.
18. Caliban, in *The Tempest*.
19. The Bastard, in *King John*.

4. Coriolanus.
5. Cordelia, in *King Lear*.
6. Thomas Mowbray, Duke of Norfolk, in *Richard II*.
7. Queen Margaret, in *Richard III*.
8. Lucius, in *Titus Andronicus*.
9. Valentine, in *The Two Gentlemen of Verona*.
10. Posthumus, in *Cymbeline*.
11. Sir John Falstaff, in *Henry IV, Part II*.
12. Belarius, in *Cymbeline*.
13. Sir John Fastolfe, in *Henry VI, Part I*.
14. Duchess of Gloucester, in *Henry VI, Part II*.
15. Earl of Kent, in *King Lear*.
16. Publius Cimber, in *Julius Caesar*.
17. Bolingbroke, Duke of Hereford, in *Richard II*.
18. Romeo, in *Romeo and Juliet*.
19. Prospero, in *The Tempest*.
20. Rosalind, in *As You Like It*.

48. "THAT OLD AND ANTIQUE SONG"

1. Silence, in *Henry IV, Part II*.
2. Sir Hugh Evans, in *The Merry Wives of Windsor*.
3. Balthasar, in *Much Ado About Nothing*.
4. Ariel, in *The Tempest*.
5. Bottom, in *A Midsummer-Night's Dream*.
6. Amiens, in *As You Like It*.
7. Lavache (Clown), in *All's Well That Ends Well*.
8. Autolycus, in *The Winter's Tale*.
9. Guiderius (Arviragus joins in later), in *Cymbeline*.
10. Fool, in *King Lear*.
11. Mercutio, in *Romeo and Juliet*.
12. Ophelia, in *Hamlet*.

13. Iago, in *Othello*.
14. Pandarus, in *Troilus and Cressida*.
15. Queen Katharine's "wench," in *Henry VIII*.
16. Stephano, in *The Tempest*.
17. Feste (Clown), in *Twelfth Night*.
18. Caliban, in *The Tempest*.
19. Pistol, in *Henry V*.
20. A Boy, in *Measure for Measure*.

49. "INSULTED, RAIL'D, AND PUT UPON"

1. Duke of Albany to Goneril, in *King Lear*.
2. Claudio to Hero, in *Much Ado About Nothing*.
3. King of France to Diana, in *All's Well That Ends Well*.
4. Isabella to Claudio, in *Measure for Measure*.
5. Thersites to Achilles, in *Troilus and Cressida*.
6. Orlando to Jaques, in *As You Like It*.
7. Antony to Cleopatra, in *Antony and Cleopatra*.
8. Antipholus of Ephesus to Adriana, in *The Comedy of Errors*.
9. Duke of Gloucester to Bishop of Winchester, in *Henry VI, Part I*.
10. Cleon to Dionyza, in *Pericles*.
11. Falstaff to Mistress Quickly, in *Henry IV, Part I*.
12. Duchess of Gloucester to Queen Margaret, in *Henry VI, Part II*.
13. Hamlet to Ophelia, in *Hamlet*.
14. Capulet to Nurse, in *Romeo and Juliet*.
15. Brutus to Cassius, in *Julius Caesar*.
16. Leontes to Camillo, in *The Winter's Tale*.
17. Constance to Duke of Austria, in *King John*.
18. Helena to Hermia, in *A Midsummer-Night's Dream*.

19. Duchess of York to Duke of York, in *Richard II*.
20. Timon to Apemantus, in *Timon of Athens*.

50. "WITH CUSTOMARY COMPLIMENT"

1. Antonio to Bassanio, in *The Merchant of Venice*.
2. Constance to Arthur, in *King John*.
3. Cressida to Troilus, in *Troilus and Cressida*.
4. Salisbury to Warwick, in *Henry VI, Part II*.
5. Hamlet to Ghost, in *Hamlet*.
6. Macbeth to Banquo's murderer, in *Macbeth*.
7. Falstaff to Mistress Ford, in *The Merry Wives of Windsor*.
8. Bolingbroke to Bishop of Carlisle, in *Richard II*.
9. Henry to Katharine, in *Henry V*.
10. Poins to Prince Henry, in *Henry IV, Part I*.
11. Goneril to *King Lear*.
12. Duke of Gloucester to Lady Anne, in *Richard III*.
13. Lucentio to Tranio, in *The Taming of the Shrew*.
14. Flavius to Timon, in *Timon of Athens*.
15. Octavius to Cleopatra, in *Antony and Cleopatra*.
16. Guiderius to Imogen, in *Cymbeline*.
17. Romeo to Tybalt, in *Romeo and Juliet*.
18. King Henry to Anne Bullen, in *Henry VIII*.
19. Tullus Aufidius to Coriolanus, in *Coriolanus*.
20. Brutus to Portia, in *Julius Caesar*.

51. "ANSWER ME IN ONE WORD"

1. "No." (*Antony and Cleopatra*)
2. "If." (*As You Like It*)
3. "Mildly." (*Coriolanus*)
4. "Amen." (*Macbeth*)

5. "Legitimate." (*King Lear*)
6. "Alone." (*Hamlet*)
7. "Choose." (*Merchant of Venice*)
8. "Pardon." (*Richard II*)
9. "Banished." (*Romeo and Juliet*)
10. "Accost." (*Twelfth Night*)
11. "Fear." (*Henry IV, Part I*)
12. "Had." (*All's Well That Ends Well*)
13. "Submission." (*Henry IV, Part I*)
14. "Accommodated." (*Henry IV, Part II*)
15. "Good." (*The Winter's Tale*)
16. "Judgment." (*Richard III*)
17. "Conscience." (*Richard III*)
18. "Rebellion." (*Henry IV, Part II*)
19. "Honour." (*Henry IV, Part I*)
20. "Farewell." (*Richard II*)

52. "O MY PROPHETIC SOUL"

1. Juliet (to Romeo), in *Romeo and Juliet*.
2. Archbishop Cranmer (about Princess Elizabeth), in *Henry VIII*.
3. Hamlet.
4. Third Witch (to Banquo), in *Macbeth*.
5. Cassius, in *Julius Caesar*.
6. John of Gaunt (about Richard), in *Richard II*.
7. Brabantio (to Othello about Desdemona), in *Othello*.
8. Charles the Dauphin, in *Henry VI, Part I*.
9. King Henry (about Earl of Richmond), in *Henry VI, Part III*.
10. Prince John, in *Henry IV, Part II*.
11. Orsino, in *Twelfth Night*.
12. Octavius Caesar, about *Antony and Cleopatra*

13. Hector, in *Troilus and Cressida*.
14. Duchess of Gloucester (about Queen Margaret), in *Henry VI, Part II*.
15. Exeter is quoting Henry V, in *Henry VI, Part I* (about Bishop of Winchester).
16. King Richard. "He" refers to Bolingbroke, and "thou" to Northumberland, in *Richard II*.
17. The Fool, in *King Lear*.
18. King John is speaking of the prophecy of Peter of Pomfret.
19. Duke of York, in *Henry VI, Part I*.
20. The Earl of Kent is prophesying his own death, in *King Lear*.

53. "A QUESTION TO BE ASKED"

1. Gremio, in *The Taming of the Shrew*.
2. Coriolanus.
3. The Bastard, in *King John*.
4. Sir Toby Belch, in *Twelfth Night*.
5. Macbeth.
6. Pandarus, in *Troilus and Cressida*.
7. Leonato, in *Much Ado About Nothing*.
8. Sir John Falstaff, in *The Merry Wives of Windsor*.
9. Juliet, in *Romeo and Juliet*.
10. Lady Percy, in *Henry IV, Part I*.
11. Porter, in *Macbeth*.
12. Petruchio, in *The Taming of the Shrew*.
13. Prince Henry, in *Henry IV, Part II*.
14. Queen Margaret, in *Henry VI, Part III*.
15. King Edward IV, in *Richard III*.
16. King Lear.
17. Brutus, in *Julius Caesar*.

18. Alcibiades, in *Timon of Athens.*
19. Hamlet.
20. Portia, in *The Merchant of Venice.*

54. "IN SELF-ADMISSION"

1. Iago, in *Othello.*
2. Mercutio, in *Romeo and Juliet.*
3. Joan la Pucelle, in *Henry VI, Part I.*
4. Cleopatra, in *Antony and Cleopatra.*
5. Hamlet.
6. Portia, in *The Merchant of Venice.*
7. Owen Glendower, in *Henry IV, Part I.*
8. Edmund, in *King Lear.*
9. Troilus, in *Troilus and Cressida.*
10. Prince Arthur, in *King John.*
11. Horatio, in *Hamlet.*
12. Autolycus, in *The Winter's Tale.*
13. King Lear.
14. Proteus, in *The Two Gentlemen of Verona.*
15. Julius Caesar.
16. Thersites, in *Troilus and Cressida.*
17. Timon of Athens.
18. Sir John Falstaff, in *Henry IV, Part II.*
19. Don John, in *Much Ado About Nothing.*
20. Petruchio, in *The Taming of the Shrew.*

55. "SUCH STUFF AS DREAMS"

1. Caliban, in *The Tempest.*
2. Cinna the Poet, in *Julius Caesar.*
3. Soothsayer, in *Cymbeline.*

4. Romeo, in *Romeo and Juliet.*
5. Duke of Clarence, in *Richard III.*
6. Duchess of Gloucester, in *Henry VI, Part II.*
7. Brabantio, in *Othello.*
8. Hermia, in *A Midsummer-Night's Dream.*
9. Tullus Aufidius, in *Coriolanus.*
10. Queen Katharine, in *Henry VIII.*
11. Shylock, in *The Merchant of Venice.*
12. Earl of Richmond, in *Richard III.*
13. Lady Macbeth, in *Macbeth.*
14. Pericles.
15. Posthumus Leonatus, in *Cymbeline.*
16. Lucullus, in *Timon of Athens.*
17. Calpurnia, in *Julius Caesar.*
18. Andromache, in *Troilus and Cressida.*
19. Cardinal Beaufort, in *Henry VI, Part II.*
20. Bottom, in *A Midsummer-Night's Dream.*

56. "KNOW YOU THIS RING?"

1. Jessica, in *The Merchant of Venice.*
2. The race to win Bianca, in *The Taming of the Shrew.*
3. Proteus, in *The Two Gentlemen of Verona.*
4. Olivia and Sebastian, in *Twelfth Night.*
5. Bassianus, in *Titus Andronicus.*
6. Fenton, in *The Merry Wives of Windsor.*
7. Lady Anne, in *Richard III.*
8. Antigonus's, in *The Winter's Tale.*
9. Portia and Nerissa, in *The Merchant of Venice.*
10. "A Gentleman" who is the agent for the Earl of Kent, in *King Lear.*
11. Simonides, in *Pericles.*

12. Viola, in *Twelfth Night.*
13. King of France, in *All's Well That Ends Well.*
14. Cranmer, in *Henry VIII.*
15. Romeo, in *Romeo and Juliet.*
16. Julia, in *The Two Gentlemen of Verona.*
17. Prince Henry, in *Henry IV, Part I.*
18. In the song that begins, "It was a lover and his lass," in *As You Like It.*
19. "A Courtezan," in *The Comedy of Errors.*
20. Posthumus, in *Cymbeline.*

57. "THUS MUCH MONEYS"

1. His "legion of angels," in *The Merry Wives of Windsor.*
2. A quart d'écu, in *All's Well That Ends Well.*
3. Three or four thousand chequins, in *Pericles.*
4. A thousand crowns, in *As You Like It.*
5. Her "purse Full of crusadoes," in *Othello.*
6. A denier, in *The Taming of the Shrew.*
7. A doit or a groat, in *Henry VI, Part II.*
8. Ten thousand dollars, in *Macbeth.*
9. Seventy-five drachmas, in *Julius Caesar.*
10. Three thousand ducats, in *The Merchant of Venice.*
11. Guilders, in *The Comedy of Errors.*
12. Thirty thousand marks of English coin, in *King John.*
13. Eight thousand nobles, in *Richard II.*
14. One noble, in *Henry VI, Part I.*
15. One penny, in *Henry IV, Part I.*
16. A thousand pounds, in *Henry VIII.*
17. Eight shillings, in *Henry V.*
18. Sixpence, in *Twelfth Night.*

19. Fifty talents, in *Timon of Athens*.
20. Three solidares, in *Timon of Athens*.

58. "A MINT OF PHRASES" Number 1

1. "Bag and baggage," in *As You Like It*.
2. "The primrose path," in *Hamlet*.
3. "We have seen better days," in *As You Like It*.
4. "Make a virtue of necessity," in *The Two Gentlemen of Verona*.
5. "Care killed a cat," in *Much Ado About Nothing*.
6. "Father Time," in *The Comedy of Errors*.
7. "Glimpses of the moon," in *Hamlet*.
8. "Journeys end," in *Twelfth Night*.
9. "As pure as snow," in *Hamlet*.
10. "Fear the worst," in *Troilus and Cressida*.
11. "Wild-goose chase," in *Romeo and Juliet*.
12. "What the dickens," in *The Merry Wives of Windsor*.
13. "Break the ice," in *The Taming of the Shrew*.
14. "Wolf in sheep's array," in *Henry VI, Part I*.
15. "We shall smile," in *Julius Caesar*.
16. "Bell, book, and candle," in *King John*.
17. "I'll not budge an inch," in *The Taming of the Shrew*.
18. "All our yesterdays," in *Macbeth*.
19. "Swim like a duck," in *The Tempest*.
20. "A swan-like end," in *The Merchant of Venice*.

59. "A MINT OF PHRASES" Number 2

1. "Poor, but honest," in *All's Well That Ends Well*.
2. "The Gordian knot," in *Henry V*.
3. "Sound and fury," in *Macbeth*.

4. "Time—must have a stop," in *Henry IV, Part I.*
5. "A twice-told tale," in *King John.*
6. "Something in the wind," in *The Comedy of Errors.*
7. "Worm will turn," in *Henry VI, Part III.*
8. "The milk of human kindness," in *Macbeth.*
9. "The man i' the moon," in *A Midsummer-Night's Dream.*
10. "Hold a candle," in *The Merchant of Venice.*
11. "Elbow-room," in *King John.*
12. "Pale cold cowardice," in *Richard II.*
13. "A fool's paradise," in *Romeo and Juliet.*
14. "Kiss me, Kate," in *The Taming of the Shrew.*
15. "Cite Scripture," in *The Merchant of Venice.*
16. "Master a grief," in *Much Ado About Nothing.*
17. "Time out o' mind," in *Romeo and Juliet.*
18. "Kill a wife with kindness," in *The Taming of the Shrew.*
19. "In such a pickle," in *The Tempest.*
20. "Good night, sweet prince," in *Hamlet.*

60. "A MINT OF PHRASES" Number 3

1. "Knit his brows," in *Henry VI, Part II.*
2. "The moon is down," in *Macbeth.*
3. "Bought and sold," in *Henry VI, Part I.*
4. "Two-headed Janus," in *The Merchant of Venice.*
5. "Like a tangled chain," in *A Midsummer-Night's Dream.*
6. "The gift of fortune," in *Much Ado About Nothing.*
7. "Pitchers have ears," in *The Taming of the Shrew.*
8. "Love me or love me not," in *The Taming of the Shrew.*
9. "To help the feeble up," in *Timon of Athens.*
10. "Westward-ho!" in *Twelfth Night.*
11. "Out-herods Herod," in *Hamlet.*
12. "Brain him," in *Henry IV, Part I.*
13. "Young and fair," in *As You Like It.*

14. "Flattered the people," in *Coriolanus.*
15. "Cut him out," in *Romeo and Juliet.*
16. "Laugh yourself into stitches," in *Twelfth Night.*
17. "She spurns my love," in *The Two Gentlemen of Verona.*
18. "Dead as a door-nail," in *Henry VI, Part II.*
19. "As poor as Job," in *Henry IV, Part II.*
20. "Great welcome," in *The Comedy of Errors.*

61. "BEING ABSENT HENCE"

1. Polyxena, in *Troilus and Cressida.*
2. Princess Elizabeth of York, in *Richard III.*
3. Maudlin, Lafeu's daughter, in *All's Well That Ends Well.*
4. Dowsabel, wife of Dromio of Ephesus, in *The Comedy of Errors.*
5. Augustus Caesar, in *Cymbeline.*
6. Lamond, in *Hamlet.*
7. Princess Mary, in *Henry VIII.*
8. Stephen Langton, in *King John.*
9. Hecuba, in *Troilus and Cressida.*
10. Hisperia, in *As You Like It.*
11. Doctor Bellario, in *The Merchant of Venice.*
12. Mistress Kate Keepdown, in *Measure for Measure.*
13. Mother Prat, the fat woman of Brentford, in *The Merry Wives of Windsor.*
14. The lord who was sent to ask Hotspur for his prisoners, in *Henry IV, Part I.*
15. Philoten, in *Pericles.*
16. Mistress Shore, in *Richard III.*
17. Fulvia, in *Antony and Cleopatra.*
18. Rosaline, in *Romeo and Juliet.*
19. Claribel, in *The Tempest.*
20. "The most pious Edward" in *Macbeth.*

PLAY BY PLAY
DEPARTMENT

62. *TROILUS AND CRESSIDA*

1. Over seven years.
2. Troilus's.
3. Agamemnon.
4. Helenus.
5. Thersites.
6. Hector.
7. An old aunt of the Trojan princes.
8. Cassandra.
9. Pandarus.
10. That Antenor be exchanged for Cressida.
11. Aeneas.
12. He is speaking of Troilus and Cressida in their farewell embrace.
13. Diomedes.
14. They all kiss her.
15. Troilus.
16. Because they are first cousins and Hector has scruples against it.
17. Ulysses.
18. A sleeve.
19. Hector's.
20. The death of Patroclus.

63. PERICLES

1. Syria.
2. By murdering them when they fail to answer a certain riddle.
3. Food, since Tarsus is having a famine.
4. Pentapolis.
5. He so distinguishes himself in a tournament that she falls in love with him.
6. Antiochus and his daughter are dead.
7. Her body must be thrown overboard.
8. Ephesus.
9. Because she was born at sea.
10. With Lychorida, Dionyza and Cleon, in Tarsus.
11. Fourteen.
12. Three pirates happen along and kidnap her from the murderer.
13. To the keeper of a brothel in Mytilene.
14. They all leave her chaste and vow to reform.
15. Lysimachus.
16. He has been shown her grave in Tarsus.
17. "The music of the spheres."
18. She faints.
19. Shave or cut his hair, or both.
20. In Pentapolis as King and Queen, Simonides having died.

64. TIMON OF ATHENS

1. Flatterers.
2. Ventidius.
3. Apemantus.
4. Ladies dressed as Amazons.
5. Apemantus.
6. Flavius.

7. Alcibiades.
8. From those he considers friends.
9. Sempronius.
10. That he has been pretending he is bankrupt to try them out.
11. None. The dishes are filled with warm water.
12. Flavius.
13. In a cave by the seashore.
14. Because Alcibiades is warring against Athens.
15. Apemantus.
16. The Poet and the Painter.
17. Flavius.
18. To help fight Alcibiades.
19. The enemies of Timon and himself.
20. By making a wax impression of it.

65. CYMBELINE

1. Cloten.
2. Posthumus Leonatus.
3. In the King's Palace.
4. Guiderius and Arviragus, Cymbeline's two sons.
5. To Rome.
6. A sort of sleeping potion.
7. "Hark, hark! the lark."
8. By producing the bracelet he stole from her arm and describing her birthmark.
9. Augustus Caesar.
10. Mulmutius.
11. Augustus Caesar.
12. Pisanio.
13. Guiderius.
14. Pisanio.
15. That of Belarius and her brothers.

16. She has taken the sleeping potion the Queen gave Pisanio.
17. He is wearing Posthumus's clothes.
18. A bloody handkerchief.
19. Guiderius, Arviragus, Belarius, and Posthumus.
20. "A mole, a sanguine star."

66. CORIOLANUS

1. Corn.
2. Menenius Agrippa.
3. Tullus Aufidius.
4. Cominius.
5. Corioli.
6. Virgilia, his wife.
7. It filled the city full of moths.
8. Because of his victory at Corioli.
9. That he is going to wash his face.
10. Because Coriolanus has forgotten his name.
11. Volumnia, his mother.
12. He thinks they are becoming to him.
13. Tarquin.
14. Exhibit his wounds to the citizens in public.
15. Adrian and Nicanor.
16. His old enemy Tullus Aufidius.
17. Sicinius Velutus and Junius Brutus.
18. That Coriolanus is leading the Volsces against them.
19. Volumnia.
20. "Boy."

67. JULIUS CAESAR

1. The feast of Lupercal.
2. Soothsayer.
3. He is deaf in his left ear.

4. Mark Antony.
5. Marcus Brutus.
6. Cicero.
7. Mark Antony, but Brutus objects.
8. Decius Brutus.
9. Trebonius.
10. Casca.
11. He flees to his house.
12. Cassius.
13. Octavius Caesar.
14. He has accused Cassius of taking bribes.
15. Marcus Brutus.
16. Marcus Brutus.
17. His sight is poor.
18. Pindarus.
19. Strato.
20. Mark Antony.

68. *ANTONY AND CLEOPATRA*

1. "A strumpet's fool."
2. By reading their palms.
3. His wife has suddenly died and Pompey has become aggressive.
4. The Ptolemies.
5. An oriental pearl.
6. Julius Caesar.
7. That Antony marry Octavia.
8. "The river of Cydnus."
9. Domitius Enobarbus.
10. That he did not make the match, but only brings the news.
11. Lepidus.
12. By describing Octavia as a most unattractive lady.

13. Octavia is to intercede for him in slights he feels.
14. He has grown too cruel and abuses his high authority.
15. Enobarbus.
16. Antony says it twice.
17. Antony.
18. Figs.
19. Yes, Charmian, and probably Iras.
20. Octavius Caesar.

69. *TITUS ANDRONICUS*

1. The Gothic Wars.
2. Alarbus, Tamora's eldest son.
3. Titus's.
4. Because she has already promised to marry Bassianus.
5. He bars the passage when Titus tries to follow Lavinia and bring her back.
6. Immediately.
7. From then on she lives for nothing but revenge on the Andronici.
8. Chiron and Demetrius.
9. Quintus and Martius.
10. They amputate her hands and tongue.
11. Marcus Andronicus.
12. By embroidering her story on a sampler. She had lost only her tongue.
13. His severed hand.
14. Ovid's "Metamorphoses."
15. Holding a staff in her mouth and guiding it with her stumps, she spells their names in the sand.
16. The Roman gods.
17. Coriolanus.
18. As a cook.

19. Four: Lavinia, Tamora, Titus, and Saturninus.
20. Lucius.

70. *AS YOU LIKE IT*

1. France.
2. Nothing.
3. At a wrestling match between Orlando and Charles.
4. He learns that Orlando is the son of a dead friend of his banished brother.
5. A chain from her own neck.
6. Duke Senior.
7. Touchstone.
8. He draws his sword and demands food.
9. Jaques.
10. Frederick orders him to find Orlando and bring him back dead or alive.
11. In a cottage they buy from a peasant.
12. He is wearing the chain that Rosalind gave him.
13. "Who ever loved that loved not at first sight?"
14. Orlando saves Oliver's life.
15. She faints.
16. Phebe.
17. "If this be so, why blame you me to love you?"
18. Touchstone.
19. Jaques de Boys.
20. Hymen, personified.

71. *THE COMEDY OF ERRORS*

1. Because traffic is forbidden between Syracuse and Ephesus and Aegeon cannot pay his ransom.
2. By their names. Ha! (See Act I, Scene I, Line 53)
3. Aegeon bought them from their poor parents.

4. Antipholus of Ephesus.

5. He has been searching for his son who left home seven years ago.

6. Solinus, Duke of Ephesus.

7. "The Centaur."

8. "The Phoenix."

9. A carcanet.

10. He is locked out of his own house.

11. To be unfaithful "by stealth."

12. Dowsabel, or Nell.

13. She describes all of his birthmarks.

14. Lapland.

15. A long one.

16. Into the Priory.

17. Her newly found mother-in-law, Aemilia.

18. Twenty-five.

19. Antipholus of Ephesus gnaws the ropes with his teeth.

20. Antipholus of Ephesus offers to ransom him, but the Duke gives him his life free.

72. LOVE'S LABOUR'S LOST

1. Three years.

2. One meal a day, and one day a week with no food at all.

3. They are to sleep only three hours a night and never show they are sleepy.

4. That the daughter of the French King is on her way to Navarre.

5. Don Adriano de Armado.

6. A "tough senior."

7. Anthony.

8. Costard.

9. Armado.

10. In Brabant.
11. To settle an old account between the King of Navarre and the ailing King of France.
12. Aquitaine.
13. Armado needs him to deliver a love letter to Jaquenetta.
14. They hunt deer.
15. Sir Nathaniel.
16. All of them.
17. "A goddess."
18. They all agree they can learn more from women's eyes than from all the books in the world.
19. Mercade enters to say the King of France is dead.
20. A year and a day.

73. *THE MERRY WIVES OF WINDSOR*

1. Beating Shallow's men, killing his deer, and breaking into his lodge.
2. Robert and Abraham, respectively.
3. "Tapster."
4. He needs money and learns the women control the purse-strings.
5. Doctor Caius, Fenton, and Slender.
6. "He is given to prayer."
7. Evans promotes Slender's suit for Anne.
8. They are exactly alike.
9. Ford.
10. When Falstaff refuses to lend him money because he refuses to deliver a letter for him.
11. Slender.
12. Fenton.
13. Because of his former association with "the wild prince" and Poins.

14. Mistress Quickly.
15. Once in a clothes basket and once disguised in a fat woman's clothes.
16. "Honest."
17. Herne the hunter.
18. "Potatoes."
19. "A great lubberly boy."
20. "I ha' married un garçon, a boy."

74. *A MIDSUMMER-NIGHT'S DREAM*

1. The wedding of Hippolyta and Theseus.
2. To die or become a nun.
3. Because she knows Demetrius will follow them, and she can follow him.
4. "The most lamentable comedy and most cruel death of Pyramus and Thisbe."
5. Peter Quince.
6. Bottom.
7. Oberon and Titania.
8. To find the magic flower, love-in-idleness, and bring it back.
9. So she will fall in love with the first creature she sees when she opens her eyes, and relinquish the changeling.
10. They are both wearing Athenian costumes.
11. Helena.
12. To see if the moon is going to shine when they present the play.
13. Puck.
14. Killing him.
15. Three.
16. By putting an antidote in his eyes.
17. His head itches all the time.

18. Onions and garlic.
19. "Moonshine."
20. Pyramus.

75. THE TAMING OF THE SHREW

1. Barthol'mew, a young page dressed as a woman.
2. An onion.
3. Because Katharina is older and must be married first.
4. Lucentio.
5. He thinks it is excellent and "would 'twere done!"
6. To see his friend Hortensio and find a rich wife.
7. Bianca's suitors and her father.
8. Because Bianca says she has no favorite suitor.
9. "I have a daughter, sir, called Katharina."
10. Because he tells her "she mistook her frets."
11. Gremio.
12. Petruchio is late for the wedding.
13. Biondello.
14. "Ay, by gogs-wouns."
15. The bride and groom leave before it begins.
16. Winter.
17. Mutton.
18. He has just refused to let his bride have a new gown and hat.
19. Old Vincentio, father to Lucentio.
20. He makes a bet that when he and two other men send for their wives, his will be the first to obey—and she is.

76. THE TEMPEST

1. Prospero produced it with his magic.
2. She had four or five women who tended her.

3. Twelve years.
4. Alonso.
5. Gonzalo.
6. His books of magic.
7. Because he sought to violate Miranda's honor.
8. Prospero.
9. Ariel guides him by singing.
10. His freedom.
11. Sebastian and Antonio.
12. England.
13. Ariel.
14. Carrying heavy logs and piling them.
15. Caliban, Stephano and Trinculo.
16. Ariel makes it vanish before they even taste it.
17. Prospero suddenly remembers the plot against his life.
18. They are spirits in the shape of dogs and hounds.
19. "Under the blossom that hangs on the bow."
20. "Brave new world."

77. *TWELFTH NIGHT*

1. They were shipwrecked.
2. As a eunuch and singer.
3. Sir Andrew Aguecheek, according to Sir Toby Belch.
4. They are both mourning for their brothers.
5. Duke Orsino.
6. To Olivia.
7. "Sebastian of Messaline."
8. Antonio, a sea captain.
9. He is too arrogant for them.
10. Maria drops it in his path as he passes by.
11. Wear yellow stockings, go cross-gartered, and smile.
12. "The bed of Ware."

13. "The Elephant."
14. Viola and Sir Andrew Aguecheek.
15. Antonio.
16. When Antonio calls her Sebastian.
17. Yes, without realizing Cesario is not the man.
18. He had a mole upon his brow.
19. Olivia.
20. "The whole pack of you."

78. THE TWO GENTLEMEN OF VERONA

1. "Homely wits."
2. Milan.
3. Julia.
4. To make Lucetta think she is not interested in him.
5. First cousins.
6. Speed.
7. Because "Love is blind."
8. Valentine, himself.
9. "Crab."
10. Thurio.
11. His "love is thaw'd."
12. The perfidious Proteus.
13. By getting his cloak away from him, which contains the rope ladder he intends to use.
14. He pretends to promote Thurio's suit.
15. That he once killed a man.
16. Musicians hired by Thurio.
17. You tell me!
18. To give his beloved dog, Crab, to Silvia.
19. Thurio.
20. By convincing the Duke their banishment should be repealed.

79. *ALL'S WELL THAT ENDS WELL*

1. "Gerard de Narbon."
2. Countess of Rousillon.
3. "A fistula."
4. To herself.
5. Parolles.
6. The Florentines and the Senoys.
7. She knows a prescription that will cure the King.
8. Lafeu.
9. The husband that she will select from among his courtiers.
10. In two days as she promised.
11. He tries to refuse, but the King orders him to obey.
12. She is to get his ring off his finger and show him a child of hers that he has fathered.
13. To Florence to enlist in the army.
14. Violenta.
15. As a pilgrim.
16. The report that Helena is dead.
17. The ring that the King had given Helena.
18. The King thinks he has murdered Helena.
19. She conspires with Diana to get Bertram's ring and to take Diana's place in a rendevouz.
20. Helena.

80. *MEASURE FOR MEASURE*

1. Angelo.
2. "The King of Hungary's."
3. Because he has been lax about the laws of the city and wants Angelo to have a free hand in enforcing them, while he looks on.
4. For anticipating marriage privileges; Juliet is with child.
5. Friar Thomas.

6. To Poland.
7. Because if a nun speaks to a man she must not show her face, or if she shows her face she must not speak.
8. Angelo's, according to Lucio.
9. Elbow.
10. "Stewed prunes."
11. Lucio.
12. That she allow Angelo to make love to her.
13. Vincentio.
14. Because her marriage-dowry was lost at sea.
15. She is to agree to Angelo's disgraceful request and then have Mariana secretly take her place.
16. At "The moated grange at Saint Luke's."
17. Lucio.
18. Because there are so many men there he has seen at Mistress Overdone's house.
19. "Remember now my brother."
20. Vincentio.

81. THE MERCHANT OF VENICE

1. To finance a trip to see the wealthy Portia so he can marry her and cancel his debts.
2. Her "sunny locks" are mentioned.
3. It was so stipulated in her father's will.
4. Her French suitor, Monsieur Le Bon.
5. At least Nerissa and Portia do.
6. Yes, most of them.
7. Three.
8. Tubal.
9. No, except a pound of flesh if he does not pay it back on time.
10. The wind changes and he leaves for Belmont.
11. Portia's picture is in it.

12. Never to tell which casket he chooses, never to marry, and to leave immediately, if he fails.
13. "The portrait of a blinking idiot."
14. Jessica.
15. That Antonio is bankrupt.
16. So that Bassanio will come into possession of all her worldly goods and can thus save Antonio from the bond.
17. To a monastery two miles away.
18. Gratiano.
19. His gloves.
20. The women.

82. MUCH ADO ABOUT NOTHING

1. Claudio.
2. "With tears."
3. Eat them.
4. Don John.
5. "The prince's jester."
6. Don John.
7. Borachio.
8. Making a match between Beatrice and Benedick.
9. Balthasar's.
10. Eavesdroppers.
11. He says he did not think he would live long enough to be married.
12. He says he has a toothache.
13. Because they can read and write.
14. They overhear a conversation between Conrade and Borachio.
15. Let him verify his reputation by stealing out of their company.
16. Margaret.
17. "Carduus Benedictus."

18. Spreading the news that she is dead.
19. Kill Claudio.
20. Borachio, under guard, confesses the whole business.

83. THE WINTER'S TALE

1. Mamillius.
2. About nine months.
3. Polixenes stays on at Hermione's invitation and not his.
4. Camillo.
5. Mamillius.
6. In prison.
7. Hermione and her supposed infidelity.
8. Antigonus.
9. To the Oracle of Delphos.
10. When his son's death is announced and the Queen faints.
11. Paulina.
12. Hermione appears to Antigonus in a vision and instructs that she be so named.
13. In a desert in Bohemia.
14. He is killed by the bear that pursues him.
15. A Bohemian shepherd.
16. Camillo.
17. The Prince is hunting a falcon which flies across the shepherd's grounds.
18. Until she sees her daughter again.
19. She is more wrinkled than he remembers her.
20. Camillo.

84. KING LEAR

1. Duke of Albany and Duke of Cornwall, respectively.
2. He plans to give the greater part of his kingdom to the one who loves him most.
3. Cordelia.

4. Earl of Kent.
5. A forged offer from Edgar of half the Earl's estate if Edmund will help murder him.
6. Forty-eight.
7. Edgar.
8. Cordelia.
9. With no followers.
10. Edgar, disguised as a madman.
11. She says: "let him smell His way."
12. Duke of Cornwall.
13. Yes.
14. Duke of Albany.
15. Edmund's.
16. Goneril poisons Regan, and then commits suicide.
17. The French lose, and Lear and Cordelia are taken prisoners by Edmund.
18. Edgar.
19. The hangman who executed Cordelia.
20. Edgar.

85. MACBETH

1. Obviously the last battle in the revolt of Macdonwald and his allies, at Fife.
2. They look like women but they have beards.
3. Macbeth will become Thane of Cawdor, then king of Scotland, and Banquo's descendants will rule.
4. Sinel.
5. As far as he knows the Thane of Cawdor is still alive.
6. Thane of Cawdor.
7. "Prince of Cumberland."
8. How long he is going to stay.
9. She alleges he looks like her father as he sleeps.
10. Macduff.

11. "Daggers."
12. At Scone.
13. Because Fleance has escaped.
14. At Colme-kill.
15. Macbeth's.
16. By murdering Macduff and his family.
17. That no man born of woman shall harm him, and that he will never be vanquished unless Birnam wood move to Dunsinane.
18. If Banquo's heirs will really rule Scotland.
19. The Prince is testing Macduff's loyalty.
20. "Earl."

86. HAMLET

1. Because of rumors that young Fortinbras is trying to regain certain lands taken by King Hamlet.
2. A tentative pastime and to be sensible about it.
3. Practice what you preach.
4. Yes, to Horatio and Marcellus.
5. The "baked-meats" left over from the funeral came in handy for the wedding.
6. Juice of hebenon.
7. Before.
8. Polonius.
9. "Southerly."
10. He is to demand an unpaid tribute.
11. There seems to be no definite reason to believe she does or does not.
12. Her love for her husband and her aversion to a second marriage.
13. When his mother screams for help, Polonius screams along with her.
14. King Claudius.

15. To urge him to fulfill his promise to avenge his murder.
16. Horatio.
17. Hamlet's father defeated Fortinbras' father.
18. Thirty years old.
19. In Ophelia's grave.
20. None.

87. ROMEO AND JULIET

1. Escalus, Prince of Verona.
2. "A crutch."
3. An illiterate servant stops Romeo on the street and asks him to read the list of guests.
4. Before.
5. By his voice.
6. Paris.
7. Because the moon is changeable.
8. Juliet.
9. He has forgotten her name.
10. Juliet's nurse and Friar Laurence. Perhaps one or two more.
11. Stop the feud between the two families.
12. He wants to cut away the part of his anatomy that contains his name.
13. The lark and the nightingale.
14. Tybalt's death.
15. At first three days, from Monday to Thursday; then her father changes it to Wednesday.
16. "Angelica."
17. The messenger was quarantined on the way.
18. Romeo.
19. He takes poison.
20. She stabs herself with Romeo's dagger.

88. OTHELLO

1. He feels slighted and revengeful because Othello has appointed Cassio his Lieutenant.
2. "Michael."
3. The Ottoman Turks.
4. Duke of Venice.
5. Twenty-eight.
6. "Honest Iago."
7. By convincing him that Cassio is his rival for Desdemona's love.
8. Both Othello and Cassio.
9. The English.
10. Montano.
11. "Any music that may not be heard."
12. Strawberries.
13. Iago.
14. A sibyl.
15. Bianca.
16. Cassio.
17. He wears a coat that protects him.
18. "Her most filthy bargain."
19. Cassio.
20. Gratiano.

89. KING JOHN

1. Arthur, son of King John's deceased elder brother Geffrey.
2. Richard, Coeur-de-lion.
3. Philip Faulconbridge, bastard son of Richard, Coeur-de-lion.
4. His mother, Queen Elinor.

5. To atone for his part in the death of Richard, Coeur-de-lion.
6. Chatillon was delayed by the wind which was blowing the wrong way.
7. Constance and Elinor.
8. By producing a will which bars Arthur.
9. Angiers.
10. That of Lewis and Blanch.
11. The Bastard.
12. Pope Innocent.
13. Stephen Langton.
14. Cardinal Pandulph.
15. By plundering the abbeys.
16. Hubert de Burgh.
17. Five moons, one of which whirls about the other four.
18. Cardinal Pandulph.
19. Prince Henry's.
20. A monk.

90. RICHARD II

1. The Duke of Gloucester's.
2. Because John of Gaunt looks so sad.
3. So he can seize his estate and clothe his soldiers for the Irish wars.
4. Because of his extravagances and his associates.
5. At Ravenspurgh.
6. Henry Percy (Hotspur).
7. He has palsy.
8. Bushy and Green.
9. To disarm if Richard will repeal his banishment and restore his property.
10. That his plants will never grow.

11. Listen to other people's woes, and then make them weep with the story of Richard's dethronement.
12. Duke of Aumerle.
13. Earl of Rutland.
14. In the taverns of London.
15. In a dungeon in Pomfret Castle.
16. His former Groom of the Stable.
17. "Barbary."
18. His jailor does not taste the food as he has been doing.
19. Abbot of Westminster.
20. Richard's body is brought to him in a coffin by Sir Pierce of Exton, his murderer.

91. HENRY IV, PART I

1. As an act of penance for the murder of Richard II.
2. Owen Glendower.
3. Hotspur.
4. Mordake Earl of Fife.
5. Sack.
6. Hangman.
7. He says the worse his behavior is now, the better he will seem by comparison when he reforms.
8. Richard II.
9. To shout "Mortimer" in his ear when he is asleep, and to give him a starling which has been taught to say nothing but "Mortimer."
10. They absent themselves from a holdup and then, disguised, rob him of his loot.
11. Hotspur.
12. "Esperance!"
13. Owen Glendower.
14. Northumberland and Glendower.

15. Falstaff.
16. The King's mistreatment of the Percy family.
17. Earl of Worcester.
18. Sir Walter Blunt.
19. To save his own life, he pretends he was struck dead in a fight with Douglas.
20. Shrewsbury.

92. HENRY IV, PART II

1. Tongues, to represent the gossipy character he is.
2. "These news" of Hotspur's defeat and death.
3. John of Lancaster and Earl of Westmoreland.
4. Lord Chief Justice.
5. Apoplexy.
6. "The young prince hath misled me."
7. Archbishop of York, Scroop.
8. Because he knows everyone would think him a hypocrite.
9. Poins' sister Nell.
10. "Speaking thick."
11. Pistol.
12. The Prince is disguised as a waiter in Boar's-Head Tavern.
13. Falstaff.
14. "Uneasy lies the head that wears a crown."
15. He orders them beheaded.
16. Thomas, Duke of Clarence.
17. He is killed in a final attempt at insurrection.
18. He is taken to the Jerusalem Chamber at Westminster to die.
19. Because the Chief Justice once imprisoned him when he was Prince of Wales.
20. Falstaff.

93. HENRY V

1. "The law Salique."
2. Archbishop of Canterbury.
3. A gift of tennis balls.
4. Nym.
5. Falstaff.
6. Duke of Exeter.
7. Lewis, the Dauphin.
8. Princess Katharine and some insignificant dukedoms.
9. The siege of Harfleur.
10. Nym.
11. Bardolph.
12. "Glove," in Act IV.
13. Agincourt.
14. Sir Thomas Erpingham.
15. Richard II.
16. Saint Crispin's day.
17. Montjoy.
18. Fluellen.
19. Pistol.
20. He has too many managers.

94. HENRY VI, PART I

1. The funeral of Henry V.
2. Henry VI, himself.
3. Duke of Bedford.
4. Sir John Fastolfe.
5. Earl of Salisbury.
6. Bastard of Orleans.
7. He has Reignier pose as the Dauphin to see if Joan knows the difference, and she does.

8. "A Talbot! a Talbot!"

9. When Talbot and his men retake Orleans after Joan had helped capture it.

10. Duke of Burgundy.

11. Countess of Auvergne.

12. Earl of Suffolk.

13. Edmund Mortimer, Earl of March.

14. As a peasant selling corn.

15. Duke of Burgundy.

16. In the Palace at Paris.

17. Bishop of Winchester.

18. Duke of York.

19. Because he is in love with her himself and cannot marry her since he already has a wife.

20. Duke of Anjou, and King of Naples and Jerusalem.

95. HENRY VI, PART II

1. Henry was not present at the ceremony, the Earl of Suffolk acting as his proxy.

2. Anjou and Maine.

3. Henry makes him the first Duke of Suffolk.

4. The Duke of Suffolk.

5. Earl of Warwick.

6. Duke of York.

7. Cardinal Beaufort and Duke of Suffolk.

8. Because the Duchess refuses to pick up the fan the Queen has dropped.

9. He accurately identifies colors.

10. Duke of Gloucester.

11. King Henry.

12. John Cade of Ashford.

13. Cardinal Beaufort.

14. He is beheaded by sailors when he tries to escape to France.

15. "Kill all the lawyers."
16. Nine months old. He mentions this several times.
17. Alexander Iden.
18. That the Duke of Somerset is in the Tower of London.
19. Lord Clifford, when he says to him, "As crooked in thy manners as thy shape!"
20. The Earl of Salisbury's.

96. HENRY VI, PART III

1. Sitting on the throne.
2. He disinherits his son and makes the Duke of York his Lord Protector and heir to the throne.
3. A paper one.
4. Lord Clifford.
5. Lord Clifford's.
6. His son Edward, Earl of March.
7. Earl of Warwick.
8. "Duke of Gloucester."
9. He is there to arrange a marriage for Edward IV with Bona.
10. That King Edward has married Lady Grey.
11. Warwick's elder daughter.
12. "Queen Elizabeth."
13. Duke of Clarence.
14. Barnet field.
15. All three of the York brothers stab him.
16. Duke of Gloucester, but King Edward stops him.
17. In the Tower of London.
18. Gloucester murders him in the Tower.
19. Her father mortgages "the Sicils" and Jerusalem and ransoms her.
20. He has a son and heir and thinks all is well with the world.

97. *RICHARD III*

1. The letter "G."
2. The Duke's given name is George.
3. Lady Anne, whom he soon marries.
4. Richmond is Stanley's step-son.
5. Queen Margaret.
6. Queen Elizabeth and her relatives.
7. Julius Caesar.
8. Mistress Shore and Queen Elizabeth.
9. Lord Hastings.
10. Because he is loyal to young Edward V.
11. By proclaiming them illegitimate.
12. Duke of Buckingham.
13. About two-thirds.
14. That Anne is dangerously ill.
15. Sir James Tyrrel.
16. Richard stalls whenever Buckingham reminds him of the promised Earldom of Hereford.
17. Elizabeth of York.
18. Lord Stanley's son George.
19. Bosworth Field.
20. The same Elizabeth of York, whom Richard had selected.

98. *HENRY VIII*

1. The Kings of England and France.
2. Cardinal Wolsey.
3. "An untimely ague."
4. Queen Katharine.
5. His Surveyor's.
6. Earl of Surrey, his son-in-law.
7. At a masked ball given by Cardinal Wolsey.

8. "No, his conscience Has crept too near another lady."
9. "Marchioness of Pembroke."
10. "Princess dowager and widow to Prince Arthur."
11. Duchess of Alençon, sister to the French King.
12. Because she is not of royal blood and, most important, she is "A spleeny Lutheran."
13. An inventory of the Cardinal's enormous wealth and a letter asking the Pope to delay the divorce.
14. Sir Thomas More.
15. Her failure to put in an appearance at the Archbishop's Court.
16. In an abbey at Leicester.
17. Griffith.
18. At Kimbolton.
19. "Primero."
20. Archbishop Cranmer.

"THE END OF THIS
DAY'S BUSINESS"

99. "THE END OF THIS DAY'S BUSINESS" Number 1

1. "Traitor to myself. (*The Comedy of Errors*)
2. "Foot-ball player." (*King Lear*)
3. "Dog will have his day." (*Hamlet*)
4. "Neither here nor there." (*The Merry Wives of Windsor*)
5. "At one fell swoop?" (*Macbeth*)
6. "The lady of the house." (*Twelfth Night*)
7. "Not to flattery!" (*Timon of Athens*)
8. "True as steel." (*A Midsummer-Night's Dream*)
9. "Shot and miss'd." (*The Taming of the Shrew*)
10. "Seem to kiss." (*Pericles*)
11. "Say, when?" (*The Merchant of Venice*)
12. "Neither rhyme nor reason?" (*The Comedy of Errors*)
13. "Die for love." (*All's Well That Ends Well*)
14. "But not for love." (*As You Like It*)
15. "His friend's infirmities." (*Julius Caesar*)
16. "Some with traps." (*Much Ado About Nothing*)
17. "Much too much." (*Henry IV, Part I*)
18. "What else?" (*Hamlet*)
19. "Too much of a good thing?" (*As You Like It*)
20. "The king's English." (*The Merry Wives of Windsor*)

100. "THE END OF THIS DAY'S BUSINESS" Number 2

1. "Give the devil his due." (*Henry IV, Part II*)
2. "Cakes and ale?" (*Twelfth Night*)
3. "Wots the miller of." (*Titus Andronicus*)
4. "And thereby hangs a tale." (*The Taming of the Shrew*)
5. "Pass away the time." (*Richard III*)
6. "Tell him to his teeth." (*Hamlet*)
7. "A woman of the world." (*As You Like It*)
8. "Eaten me out of house and home." (*Henry IV, Part II*)
9. "It was Greek to me." (*Julius Caesar*)
10. "A threatening eye." (*King John*)
11. "Tell truth, and shame the devil!" (*Henry IV, Part I*)
12. "To boot." (*Troilus and Cressida*)
13. "Sink or swim." (*Henry IV, Part I*)
14. "Smells to heaven." (*Hamlet*)
15. "One too many?" (*The Comedy of Errors*)
16. "No man but myself." (*Timon of Athens*)
17. "Let the world slide." (*The Taming of the Shrew*)
18. "Every mother's son." (*A Midsummer-Night's Dream*)
19. "Such as it is." (*Hamlet*)
20. "One not sociable." (*Cymbeline*)